C0-AOD-801

International comparisons of energy consumption

Proceedings of a workshop sponsored by Resources for the Future and the Electric Power Research Institute

JOY DUNKERLEY, editor

RESEARCH PAPER R-10

RESOURCES FOR THE FUTURE / WASHINGTON, D.C.

ACKNOWLEDGMENT OF SUPPORT AND LEGAL NOTICE

The workshop on International Comparisons of Energy Use was financed by the Electric Power Research Institute (EPRI) of Palo Alto, California. The findings and conclusions, however, are those of the authors and not of EPRI or any of its member organizations.

In keeping with its policies, EPRI also makes the following legal notice:

"This report was prepared by Resources for the Future as an account of work sponsored by the Electric Power Research Institute, Inc. ("EPRI"). Neither EPRI, members of EPRI, nor Resources for the Future, nor any person acting on behalf of either:

"a. Makes any warranty or representation, express or implied, with respect to the accuracy, completeness, or usefulness of the information contained in this report, or that the use of any information, apparatus, method, or process disclosed in this report may not infringe privately owned rights; or

"b. Assumes any liabilities with respect to the use of, or for damages resulting from the use of, any information, apparatus, method, or process disclosed in this report."

Library of Congress Catalog Card Number 78-4334
ISBN 0-8018-2129-0

Copyright © 1978 by Resources for the Future, Inc.

Manufactured in the United States of America

Published April 1978. $7.50.

333. 7
I 61

RESOURCES FOR THE FUTURE, INC.
1755 Massachusetts Avenue, N.W., Washington, D.C. 20036

Board of Directors:
Gilbert F. White, *Chairman,* Irving Bluestone, Harrison Brown, Roberto de O. Campos, William T. Coleman, Jr., Luther H. Foster, F. Kenneth Hare, Charles J. Hitch, Charles F. Luce, George C. McGhee, Ian MacGregor, Laurence I. Moss, Frank Pace, Jr., Emanuel R. Piore, Stanley H. Ruttenberg, Lauren Soth, Janez Stanovnik, Julia D. Stuart, Robert D. Stuart, Jr., Russell E. Train, P. F. Watzek.

Honorary Directors: Horace M. Albright, Erwin D. Canham, Edward J. Cleary, Hugh L. Keenleyside, Edward S. Mason, William S. Paley, John W. Vanderwilt

President: Charles J. Hitch

Vice President: Emery N. Castle

Secretary-Treasurer: John E. Herbert

Resources for the Future is a nonprofit organization for research and education in the development, conservation, and use of natural resources and the improvement of the quality of the environment. It was established in 1952 with the cooperation of the Ford Foundation. Grants for research are accepted from government and private sources only if they meet the conditions of a policy established by the Board of Directors of Resources for the Future. The policy states that RFF shall be solely responsible for the conduct of the research and free to make the research results available to the public. Part of the work of Resources for the Future is carried out by its resident staff; part is supported by grants to universities and other nonprofit organizations. Unless otherwise stated, interpretations and conclusions in RFF publications are those of the authors; the organization takes responsibility for the selection of significant subjects for study, the competence of the researchers, and their freedom of inquiry.

TABLE OF CONTENTS

FOREWORD

Not long after the energy price rise of 1973/74 had begun to focus
attention on energy conservation, we became interested at RFF in the question, "Why is per capita consumption of energy so much higher in the United
States than it is in other advanced European countries whose per capita
income and living standards do not differ appreciably from the United
States?" Thanks to financial support from the Electric Power Research
Institute (EPRI) we were able to make a detailed though by no means exhaus-
tive study of this question for a number of industrialized countries for
the year 1972. The results were published recently as a book entitled
How Industrial Societies Use Energy, by J. Darmstadter, J. Dunkerley, and
J. Alterman (Baltimore, Johns Hopkins University Press for Resources for the
Future, 1977).

In the course of this study we became aware of numerous individuals and
groups, both in this country and abroad, who were involved in analyzing
various aspects of the same question. As many researchers were unaware that
similar work was going on elsewhere, the idea of a small meeting to enable
specialists working in the field to acquaint each other with their approaches
and results was very appealing. Again, EPRI provided both financial support
and encouragement. In particular, EPRI's President, Dr. Chauncey Starr,
demonstrated a lively interest in the project from its inception.

While agreeing that international energy comparisons could be useful in
demonstrating flexibility in energy use, in helping to identify areas of
conservation potential, and in illustrating the effects of differing price
levels on energy consumption, the participants were, on the whole, cautious
in making sweeping generalizations about what foreign experience implies

for U.S. conservation policies. By keeping this volume shorter than the usual workshop proceedings, we hope to bring this spirit of sober assessment, including an appreciation of the complexity inherent in such comparisons, to a wider audience.

Special mention must be made of the role played, on RFF's behalf, by Joy Dunkerley. Coaxing the participants to write discussion papers, to attend the meeting, and to put together this volume was not an easy assignment, even though she brought to it the familiarity with the subject matter gained in research on the above-cited RFF book. While the other participants are well identified in the pages that follow, it is my pleasure to highlight her role in this preface.

Hans H. Landsberg
Co-Director,
Center for Energy Policy Research

March 1978

WORKSHOP ACKNOWLEDGMENTS

Many people assisted in the planning and conduct of this workshop.
It benefited at all stages from the tireless enthusiasm of Chauncey Starr,
president of the Electric Power Research Insitute, which bore the cost of the
workshop. Other EPRI staff, in particular Rene Males, Richard Rudman, and
Rex Riley (the EPRI project manager) gave helpful advice and support.

At Resources for the Future, Debbie Hemphill and Linda Sanford were
responsible for much of the material organization, and their efficiency
contributed greatly to the smooth running of the workshop. Other RFF
colleagues--Jack Alterman, Joel Darmstadter, Lincoln Gordon, Jack Schanz,
Sam Schurr--gave most generously of their time, as did Charles Hitch, RFF's
president.

In the end a workshop can only be as successful as its participants,
and we were extremely fortunate in this respect. Although it was put together
at very short notice, papers were prepared and revised on time. The enthusiasm
and forbearance of the participants was reflected in the stimulating panel
discussion.

Finally, the preparation of this document was expedited by the assistance
of Linda Sanford, Radford Schantz, and Marjorie Montgomery.

SUMMARY OF WORKSHOP CONCLUSIONS

Comparisons of energy consumption between the United States and other industrialized countries <u>can be</u> useful guides for U.S. policy making in a number of ways:

> They demonstrate that there can be differing amounts of energy use for given levels of output, and indicate sectors which might be worth further investigation to determine conservation potential.

> They illustrate the effects of different energy prices. Experience abroad with price levels much higher than those faced by the United States provides an opportunity for examining effects of different price levels on energy consumption.

> They can theoretically throw light on policy implementation as well as formulation. By observing the experience of other countries, it may be possible to see which combination of price incentives and regulatory or institutional interventions promises success.

Such comparisons <u>are not</u> useful guides for U.S. policy making when they are used, as they frequently are, to imply that this country could quickly reduce energy consumption to European levels with minimum loss of welfare. This type of gross comparison does not take into account differences in economic and physical structure, or in prices of energy and other inputs among countries.

BACKGROUND TO THE WORKSHOP

This workshop is one of a series of projects concerning international comparisons of energy consumption undertaken jointly by EPRI and RFF. The first project analyzed energy consumption relative to Gross Domestic Product (GDP) for a group of advanced industrialized countries in one year (1972). This study, entitled How Industrial Societies Use Energy, was published in December 1977. A second, at present underway, will analyze trends in energy/output ratios for the same countries over time.

The joint interest of EPRI, RFF, and the other workshop participants in international energy comparisons seems in retrospect to have been very prescient. Almost any speech on energy conservation these days quotes the example of countries which use less energy relative to output than the United States. President Carter's National Energy Plan, for example, refers to the greater U.S. use of energy per dollar of Gross National Product compared with any other industrialized nation, and even devotes one whole page to a diagrammatic representation. In a recent news conference (October 13, 1977) the president again drew attention to "wasteful" habits in the United States.[1] A subject which started as a somewhat esoteric field of investigation is now being brought into the policy-making process.

The growing number of comparative studies being made both here and abroad and the way in which they are being used in policy declarations provided the impetus for organizing a meeting of persons with extensive experience in

---

[1]"We are simply wasting too much energy. For the same standard of living we use twice as much energy as is used in Japan, West Germany, Sweden and other countries of that kind. So we have got to cut down on our waste through conservation measures, voluntary action and a realization of the seriousness of this question."

the field. It was hoped to find out, during the course of such a meeting, what work was being done, what additional work needed to be done, and finally, how to interpret the results.

The organization of the workshop reflected these concerns, devoting the first day to an exchange of information on results and methods, starting with a panel overview of existing studies. Then, since the comparison of energy consumption among countries usually raises formidable data and measurement problems, a separate panel discussed these two important topics.

Rather than limit the workshop to results and technical aspects of international studies, it was decided to use international comparisons as a springboard for discussing potentialities for energy conservation in the United States in the three major energy-consuming sectors--buildings, transport, and industry. The third panel addressed these issues. Another session discussed the importance of government policy in affecting energy consumption. The final session was devoted to the use and limitations of international energy consumption comparisons. Results were assessed in order to see their relevance for conservation policy. This volume is designed to capture the essence of both the formally presented papers and the discussions while remaining short enough and general enough to appeal to an audience wider than that of the specialists who attended the workshop.

The proceedings have been summarized in the first section, drawing on both the content of the papers presented and the discussion which followed. It was hoped to summarize all nineteen of the workshop papers in the second section, but several of these papers reported for the first time results of new research, or new analysis not generally available elsewhere. Those papers (by Starr, Doernberg, Griffin, Fishelson-Long, Van Vactor, and Gordon) have therefore been reproduced in their entirety. For the other papers, a summary long enough to give a good indication of their content and conclusions has been included. For those wishing further information, complete versions of the paper are available either from the authors or from Resources for the Future.

SUMMARY OF THE WORKSHOP

Joy Dunkerley
Resources for the Future

The Nature of the Studies

Three broad types of studies comparing international energy consumption patterns can be distinguished: (1) sectoral analyses, (2) input-output analyses, and (3) econometric analyses.

Sectoral analyses, which formed the largest number of the studies presented at the workshop (Darmstadter, Johnson, Schipper, White, Doernberg), typically take the energy/GDP ratios of two or more countries, of which one is the United States, in a given year and proceed to disaggregate energy consumption as far as possible. Included in this category is the paper by Starr, which compares energy/GDP ratios among the individual states of the United States, rather than sectors between countries. The minimum level of disaggregation in the studies was transport, industry, residential/commercial, nonenergy, and transformation losses where appropriate. (If transformation losses, in practice mainly heat losses sustained in electricity generation, were distributed among the forgoing sectors, they would naturally not be distinguished as a separate sector.) Most studies managed a further degree of disaggregation, such as dividing transport into passenger and freight transport, and individual industries.

Within each sector or subsector an attempt was made to distinguish between structural differences and energy intensity differences. "Structure" (or inter-country heterogeneity) covers a wide variety of factors such as size of industrial sector, importance of energy-intensive industries in the industrial sector, differences in product mix, vintage of energy-using capital stocks, climate, population density, propensity to travel, policies affecting use of energy and other input factors, and life-style attributes such as the premium people place on time or on personal comfort. "Intensity" in this context refers to the amounts of energy used in producing reasonably homogeneous goods or carrying out similar activities. The interest in identifying the different amounts of energy needed to perform the same function--that is, the intensity characteristic--is to see if a particular mix of goods and services could be produced with a different (lower) consumption of energy. If it can be shown, for example, that Europeans can produce a ton of steel or travel a passenger mile with less energy than Americans, this could have implications for U.S. conservation policies.

Differences in structure among countries go to the heart of the question of the usefulness of international comparison. If such differences of structure cannot be systematically sorted out, then it is difficult to make valid international comparisons. In such circumstances like would not be compared with like. Much of the workshop discussion centered on whether it was possible to identify separate structural elements. Some of the structural differences, such as climate, are relatively easy to account for, though even here difficulties have been encountered. Others are not so easy to account for either because of data deficiencies or their inherently unquantifiable nature.

As an example of data deficiencies, one of the major differences between countries in the industrial area may be in the vintage of capital stock. The faster growth rate of many European countries in the past twenty years has resulted in European countries now having a more up-to-date and possibly more energy-efficient capital stock than the United States. Certainly in several of the individual products studied--iron and steel, cement--the higher U.S. consumption was related to the more predominant use of older technologies--the open-hearth furnace and wet cement process. Although information on vintage of capital stock can be of major importance for energy

conservation, the absence of reliable data means that this factor cannot
be included in quantitative international comparisons.

An example of the second difficulty--that some intercountry differences
are inherently unquantifiable--is differences in taste and life-style.[1]
People have different tastes with regard to comfort and time, which considerably
affect the way they use energy. Such differences can impair the homogeneity
necessary for intensity comparisons. Thus a passenger-mile may be traveled
in greater or lesser comfort while polluting the atmosphere to a greater or
lesser extent.

A major advantage of the sectoral approach over the others is that
the energy and sectoral activity level data necessary for an initial sectoral
breakdown are available, so that preliminary estimates of intercountry
differences can be quickly developed.

The disadvantage is that most of the studies done so far apply only to
to one year, typically 1972. This leaves them vulnerable to the criticism
that things have changed since 1972 (although in fact there is little
evidence to suggest that the _relative_ positions of the United States and
other countries have in fact changed). It also means that trends and time-
related factors influencing energy/GDP ratios are not taken into account. For
example, in 1972 one country with a high energy/GDP ratio might be on a falling
trend while another country with a low energy/GDP ratio in that year might be
on a rising trend. A comparison of energy/GDP ratios several years later
might therefore show different results.

Furthermore, it was pointed out that in one sense the distinction
between structural and intensity factors, a feature of all the sectoral

---

[1]Some attempts to quantify differences in life-style were reported. See
Chauncey Starr paper, page 25.

studies, was not clear-cut because both are affected by the same variables, notably price changes. There is some expectation, however, that with any given price change, "intensity" may be more rapidly amenable to change than physical, geographical, and historical characteristics.

The sectoral studies have the additional disadvantage that the comparison of a small number of countries in one year inhibits systematic analysis of the effects of price changes on energy consumption, a factor universally felt to be of major importance.

Moreover, a country-by-country comparison is weak in the sense that one country, say the United States, is being compared with another whose energy consumption is lower, but which may itself have considerable potential for energy conservation. The comparative approach gives only a partial indication of the potential for energy conservation. For example, the comparison of heating practices in buildings between the United States and the United Kingdom obscures the fact that in both cases insulation practices may leave much room for improvement.

To remedy this particular deficiency, three presentations (Hirst, Goodson, and Spencer) focused on energy conservation potential in the United States on its own merits, that is, without reference to other countries. Typically, the estimates of energy conservation potential derived from intracountry studies are larger than those derived from intercountry comparisons because the latter reflect imperfect energy-using habits abroad.

A final limitation of the sectoral approach is that for the industrial sector, at least, it is unwieldy and could be a misleading way of identifying industrial energy conservation strategy. That is, if a careful comparison of energy use in a specific industrial process is needed, the best way to go about it is to study that process directly, without need of prior dis-aggregation from highly aggregated totals.

The input-output studies provide a neat way to summarize a number of features of international comparisons. The studies presented here (Alterman, Smolik) were used to make the distinction between structural and intensity factors, though in a way somewhat different from the sectoral studies. In the I-O system, "structure" refers to the difference in the detailed categories of final demand, while "intensity" includes not only direct, but also indirect energy consumed in a given activity. This last characteristic offers a major advantage because it captures the entire energy cost of a given end use. This can differ considerably from the direct use given by the sectoral approach. It should be noted that the study reported by Smolik, although discussed in an international setting, was not designed for international comparison, but rather to identify within countries energy-intensive industries and the energy content of final demands. The RFF study, on the other hand, was designed as an international study, but was a partial approach combining other countries' bills of goods with U.S. input-output coefficients.

Both practical and conceptual problems are encountered in making international comparisons through input-output techniques. On a practical level, these include standardization of accounting systems and levels of aggregation among countries' input-output tables. In many countries, for example, the electricity and gas sector also includes water and sanitary services. Other problems are that input-output tables are published only infrequently and with a substantial time lag. On a conceptual level, relative prices (including taxes) differ among countries so that differences in final demand structure and input-output coefficients may reflect differences in price structure. Furthermore, differences in technological coefficients among countries may reflect not only relative prices but also differences in product mix.

Two econometric studies (Griffin, Fishelson and Long) were presented at the workshop.[2] Griffin's study, modeling the energy demand of eighteen OECD countries, is designed to show the effects of fuel prices on substitution between energy and nonenergy goods, and on substitution between fuels. In addition, the model relates the effects of economic activity on the mix and level of energy consumption. The object of the model is to provide the policy analyst with the ability to vary assumptions on both fuel prices and economic growth and then measure their impact on energy consumption. Fishelson and Long's study analyzes factor substitutability in the iron and steel industry of the United States and several other industrialized countries.

These approaches, by incorporating prices of energy, and sometimes prices of other factors of production, have the advantage of modeling industrial energy consumption in the context of overall economic efficiency rather than merely energy efficiency.

On the other hand, the econometric studies, like the sectoral studies, encounter difficulties in dealing with inherently unquantifiable differences among countries or with differences for which there are inadequate data.

Technical Questions

This, then, is a brief description of the types of studies presented at the workshop, along with their main advantages and disadvantages. In addition, there was a broad range of problems common to all studies. The first were associated with measuring output among countries. Almost all were agreed on the importance of converting GDP--the output side of the energy/GDP ratio--to a comparable unit using purchasing power parity rates of exchange rather than

---

[2]Note that the econometric papers also provide a method for estimating the input-output coefficients as a function of price.

exchange rates, despite the fact that purchasing power parities themselves are approximate. While this had long been the favored solution in theory, it has become more practicable in recent years due to the UN International Comparisons Project (Sachse) series of studies calculating purchasing power parities for different countries. The workshop also heard about a related study by the Union Bank of Switzerland (Cahill and Hermann).

In practice, the use of purchasing power parity ratios rather than exchange rates reduces the apparent difference in income levels between the United States and other countries, the reduction being much greater for countries with relatively low nominal GDP expressed in exchange rates. This adjustment was particularly important for the studies done in 1972 when the difference between GDPs expressed at market exchange rates and purchasing power parity ratios was as much as 20 percent. Since then, with the general shift toward floating exchange rates, market rates for developed countries have moved in the direction of purchasing power parity and the difference between the two has much diminished.

This raises the question of whether for comparisons involving developed countries only it is still necessary to invest the considerable effort it takes to develop purchasing power parity ratios. Will not the closely converging and more available market exchange rates serve as well? The answer is not entirely. While the floating of recent years has diminished the gap, floating exchange rates are not entirely "free" or "clean"; moreover, exchange rates reflect internationally traded goods only, whereas purchasing parities apply to all goods, including the major portion which does not enter international trade. And for developing countries the differences between purchasing power parities and exchange rates continue to be much more pronounced.

Second, there was some discussion as to the necessity for correcting energy consumption data for fuel mix. As one participant put it, "we have been treating energy as though it is a homogeneous output, a rose is a rose is a rose, a Btu is a Btu is a Btu." The Btu measure of fuel value is appropriate for processes involving low temperature heat, but comparisons of primary energy use for other types of conversion, such as from potential energy to mechanical motion, high temperature heat, or light, are poorly served by this measure. Even for applications with heat as an end function, the simple calorimetric comparisons do not take into account the use efficiency of the entire system. An example given was that of the energy potential of a high mountain lake which can be converted to electricity with 90 percent efficiency, delivered with 91 percent efficiency, and used to generate heat with 100 percent efficiency (or more if a heat pump is used). This 82 percent system efficiency is substantially higher than the efficiencies found in any fossil fuel system. It is theoretically possible to weight the value of each fuel by a factor which reflects the aggregate of end use functions (some attempt is made along these lines in the Griffin paper and in part of the RFF studies), but such a factor is of course inappropriate for any one specific end use comparison.

Finally, there was considerable discussion of the data base. The sectoral studies have benefited from data on energy consumption, GDP, and industrial production already collected by international organizations and have in turn contributed to the collection and development of data in other fields, partic- ularly transportation and housing (see Carhart presentation of WAES). Further extension of this work, for example, to greater disaggregation of the industry sector, distinction between intercity and intracity traffic, or analysis of office space in the commercial sector, is greatly handicapped by lack of data. The extension of input-output analyses is also dependent on additional data.

Econometric studies encounter considerable problems because of their formidable
data requirements for prices of energy and other factors of production. The
prospect appears to be no better for surveys of energy use within the United
States. Further work is critically dependent on data availability, which
in turn depends on the initiatives of government agencies here and abroad.

The Results of the Studies

Given the diversity of background, training, and interest of those
who have conducted the sectoral studies, the results were surprisingly
similar. After accounting as well as possible for structural differences
among countries, energy intensities were found to differ significantly,
in particular between the United States and other countries. Most, but not
all, of the activity and industrial processes distinguished indicated that
the United States used more energy than other countries. The differences
were particularly marked in passenger transport and industrial processes.
In those studies which included cold weather countries, there was also a
marked difference in the amounts of energy consumed in heating buildings.

However, there were areas where the United States compared favorably
with other countries. An example quoted by several participants was freight
transport. In this case the United States uses less energy than many other
countries because of the large amounts of freight which move on energy-efficient
systems such as railroads, barges, and pipelines.

It was agreed in general that these results demonstrated a considerable
flexibility in energy use among countries and were highly suggestive of
energy conservation potential for the United States. First, they could
be used to identify the most promising areas of energy conservation potential.
In terms of sectoral analysis, this would be in the areas of greatest
differences between the United States and other countries, that is, passenger
transport, buildings, industrial processes. Second, such studies could be

useful in illustrating the potential _amounts_ of energy conservation. It
could be argued on the basis of these studies, for example, that even if
Americans kept their reliance on the private automobile and continued to
have a greater propensity for road travel than Europeans, important savings
(about 6 percent of total energy consumption) could be achieved by improving
the fuel efficiency of cars to European levels. Similarly, the studies
permit some _screening_ of conservation potential by identifying those areas
where intensity differences between the United States and other countries
for a given activity may be large, but where the quantity of energy used in
that activity is relatively small, therefore limiting the conservation potential.
An example was rapid rail transit, where some speakers doubted that it was
worthwhile undertaking the large capital expenditures entailed by many mass
transit schemes and trying to change travel habits which in the past had
proved resistant to change, in order to achieve relatively small energy savings.

A further conclusion common to all of the sectoral studies was that
prices played a major role in determining differences in energy consumption
among countries. Thus, all studies found prices faced by consumers in
all sectors--residential, industrial, and transport--to be much lower in the
United States than in Western Europe and Japan. This suggests that energy
conservation does occur in response to price changes. Most authors of
sectoral analyses drew attention to differences in government pricing policies
as they may affect energy. The variation in prices themselves owes much to
much higher taxes on petroleum products imposed in Western European countries.
Furthermore, some countries of Western Europe impose heavy taxes on automobiles
and enforce much more stringent standards for building insulation.

Finally, authors drew attention to the limitations of their studies,
especially with regard to broad policy aims such as economic efficiency,
freedom of choice, or full employment. While reductions in energy consumption

may not necessarily conflict with these policy aims, these studies did not for the most part address this problem directly.

The input-output and econometric studies presented at the meeting generally emphasized methodology rather than results. The input-output analysis contained in the RFF study confirmed the results of the sectoral studies, namely, the higher intensity of energy use in the United States than in other industrial countries, after taking into account different "structural" characteristics.

The Economic Commission for Europe (ECE) input-output study, however, focused on identifying energy-intensive sectors within a series of countries rather than on international comparisons. Nonetheless, in the course of this exercise some conclusions of relevance to international comparisons were made. As might be expected, the study showed that in all countries energy itself is the most energy-intensive sector. Large amounts of energy are needed by this sector because of the high losses involved in the conversion of energy (particularly to electricity) and from the large use of energy in the extraction, transportation, and distribution of fuels. From the conservation point of view, the shifting in structure of final demand away from energy-intensive products has the added advantage of saving the energy needed to produce the energy which is directly saved.

Second, the ECE paper drew attention to the difference in structure of energy consumption between the United States and European countries. Typically, about 30 percent of energy consumption in European countries goes to private consumption, while U.S. private consumption accounts for more.

The econometric studies of Fishelson-Long and Griffin approached energy conservation potentials by evaluating the extent of substitution between energy and other inputs. The debate on these studies included additional reference to the growing literature on this subject concerning

substitution possibilities over time in the U.S. manufacturing sector. The
workshop discussions centered on whether energy and capital should be
considered complements, as indicated by the results of intracountry studies,
or substitutes, which appeared to result from international cross-sectional
studies such as Griffin's. The conclusions appear to be that in some cases,
in some industries, they may be complements, and in others, substitutes; and
that the overall result will depend on which predominates.

Capital and energy should be viewed together as a bundle within which
capital and energy can substitute for each other. All studies can accept
capital and energy as substitutes in this sense. This bundle of capital and
energy is then a substitute for other inputs, in particular labor. The
substitutability between the capital-energy bundle and labor may, for example,
dominate any intrabundle substitutability, making it appear, because capital
and energy inputs are both increasing, that they are in fact, complements.
In general, it seemed that further definitional work is needed before final
results can be reported on these issues, since results on complementarity
of substitution between energy and capital can depend in some cases on
measurement techniques.

Policy Formulation and Implementation

Since the main focus of the workshop was the presentation of sectoral
studies, the discussion of the use of international studies as guidelines
to policy formulation and implementation in the United States centered on
these studies. As already noted, the participants agreed that these studies
showed a variation in energy use among countries which was useful in identifying
areas of potential conservation. Differences in prices and energy policies
suggested that these factors played a major role in determining the intensity
of energy consumption. This raises the question of how far these results can
justifiably be used in policy formulation.

The participants agreed on one conclusion which, though negative, is nonetheless important. This was that the aggregate energy/GDP when compared among countries is unsuitable as a guideline for policy formulation, since it is an unsatisfactory measure of either economic efficiency or energy efficiency. With regard to economic efficiency, the energy/GDP ratio is unsatisfactory because energy is only one input--and quantitatively a small one at that--into the total of goods and services which represents GDP. Capital, labor, and other materials inputs are much larger. Societies, industries, and firms combine these factors in different ways. The amount of energy inputs or consumption in a country will be affected by the price of energy relative to the prices of the other inputs which can be substituted for energy and other factors such as differences in technology, resource base, and industrial mix. There is, in short, no universally "right" amount of energy consumption, only that which is appropriate to the configuration of economic and other factors in a particular country.

Neither is the overall energy/GDP ratio a good indicator of energy efficiency, since the amount of energy consumed in a country relative to GDP is affected by the industrial composition of the economy. A country whose economic activities are concentrated in energy-intensive industry will consume more energy than a country whose economic activities are concentrated in agriculture.[3] In both cases energy may be used with exemplary efficiency throughout the economy, but this will not stop the energy/GDP ratio of the industrial economy from being much higher than that of the agricultural economy. On these grounds there was near unanimous agreement that the overall

---

[3] The calculated difference between the energy/GDP ratios of the two countries could of course be diminished by including energy embodied in (nonenergy) foreign trade, on the assumption that the industrial economy is exporting energy-intensive goods and importing less energy-intensive goods; and that the agricultural economy is doing the reverse.

energy/GDP ratio when compared among countries was misleading and certainly did not provide good guidance for conservation policy. The best that can be said is that it is less misleading than comparisons of total or per capita energy consumption or its changes.

There was some feeling that the overall energy/GDP ratio measured over time within a country could provide more useful means of monitoring progress in conservation.[4] Indeed, this is one of the indicators used by the International Energy Agency in its annual reports on member countries' conservation programs. An analogy was suggested between the movement of the energy/GDP ratio over time and indices such as the unemployment rate or the Dow Jones average. While the latter two could be criticized on all sorts of grounds-- for obscuring variations at a lower level of aggregation or for not taking into account structural changes in the economy--they nonetheless provided unique and useful information. On similar grounds, it was suggested that for all its faults the energy/GDP ratio could provide a degree of useful information. It was also pointed out that the aggregate energy/GDP ratio might be more consistent than the disaggregated data, as countries frequently change categories of energy use. In this event, results which appear at first sight to indicate changes in sectoral energy efficiency merely reflect recategorization of energy demand.

On the other hand, the overall energy/GDP ratio is often an unsatisfactory indication of energy efficiency over the short run because changes in level of economic activity can lead to substantial year-to-year changes in the energy/GDP ratio. Furthermore, it may be strongly influenced by changing fuel mix.

----

[4]The rationale behind the use of energy/GDP ratios over time but not among countries is that over time technology, industrial composition, and other structural features do not show as much variation as they do between countries.

The general conclusion was that while the aggregate energy/GDP ratio was an unsatisfactory measure of comparative energy or economic efficiency among countries, it might have value in judging a country's behavior over time, but only when viewed as a longer term trend rather than from year to year.

Given the virtual unanimity of this group of specialists on the misleading nature of aggregate energy/GDP comparisons among countries, it is remarkable that energy/GDP ratios are widely quoted by politicians, by the press, and by the public at large and show every indication of playing some role in energy policy decision making. As one participant put it,

> None of us who spoke this morning failed to preface his remarks by pointing out that aggregates mean nothing and no inferences should be drawn on these broad energy/GDP comparisons, yet there abounds in the land nothing but energy/GDP comparisons. So I am sort of curious----if we are all agreed that this is a misguided way to make inter- national comparisons, somebody is at fault. I would go so far as to render the judgment that those who are at fault don't exclude the scientific community----it is not only unsophisticated people who are exploiting these aggregates which we unanimously say in a chorus we should not use.

The answer appears to be that whatever its faults in the eyes of the specialists, the aggregate energy/GDP ratio provides a convenient short expression, easy for policy makers and the public alike to understand, and at times perhaps to exploit for subjective reasons. There is clearly an opportunity here for the specialists to urge caution on those who would use overall energy/GDP ratios to make sweeping generalizations about possibilities of energy conservation.

Having dismissed the use of the aggregate energy/GDP ratio as a useful guide to policy formulation, the workshop participants felt that international comparisons, particularly on the sectoral level, could indeed be useful for policy making in a number of ways (Gordon).

The first has already been referred to. At a minimum, serious international comparisons are suggestive, demonstrating that there can be differing degrees of energy intensity for given levels of output and pointing toward the sectors which might be worth further investigation to determine conservation potential. This role of international comparison is indicative and qualitative, rather than precise and quantitative, and should be supplemented by analyses dealing directly with specific American conditions.

Another role of international comparisons is to illustrate the example of different energy price levels. Most other industrial countries have had many more years of experience with higher energy costs and prices than the United States. In this sense, a series of laboratories are available for examining the effects of different price levels. They are admittedly not clean laboratories, and they do not permit the kind of controlled experimentation used by the physical sciences. Nevertheless, actual experience abroad with price levels much higher than those faced by the United States[5] is surely superior to the extrapolations in some studies based on very small differentials within a single country.

It must be remembered, however, that the lessons to be drawn from areas with higher energy prices must be tempered by a recognition of the long time period which may be involved in adjusting energy consumption. The existence of a low level of consumption in one particular activity in one country may not be a good guide to what can be achieved in another country in the short to medium term, because the pattern of low consumption may have been established over many years of high prices. As was emphasized repeatedly during the workshop, large improvements in energy efficiencies in industry

---

[5]According to RFF estimates, U.S. prices have moved in the direction of, rather than arrived at, European levels. In the years before 1973, U.S. energy prices were on the whole half of the level of European prices; after the OPEC price increase of 1974 they moved up in real terms by 30-40 percent. The gap has narrowed but not closed (pushing the United States partially in that direction). In the meantime, of course, Western European energy prices have risen by similar amounts so that the relative difference between the two price levels has not changed much.

do not occur overnight. There exists a whole spectrum of conservation oppor-

tunities or opportunities for improving the efficiency of energy utilization.

These begin with housekeeping improvements, better maintenance programs,

patching up leaky steam lines, changing practices on heating or cooling

unused space, all of which generally take relatively small amounts of capital

and can be put into effect on a relatively short time scale, even if not

immediately. Then there are improvements that require replacing specific

items of equipment or substantial changes in operating procedures. Finally,

others require major capital expenditures, construction, and redesign of

production processes, which generally take a long time. International

comparisons may therefore indicate a large conservation potential in the

long run which may not be relevant if a country's policy aims are focused

on the near to medium term.

Behind the results of higher prices lies the question of how those

results were achieved. At several points in the workshop attention was

drawn to the analytic differences between energy consumption in intermediate

uses, that is manufacturing, and energy consumption in final demand uses,

particularly by households. It was considered that the set of forces that

operate on a producer's choice of factor inputs, for example, in the production

of aluminum ingot between West Germany and the United States, is quite

different from the forces that would be needed to explain the demand for

gasoline, the acquisition of cars, or behavior toward home insulation. To

examine such final demand components of energy consumption, it is necessary

not only to probe the purely economic determinants of behavior but the whole

panoply of instutitional-attitudinal-behavioral factors. Participants felt

that the intermediate sector would be generally well aware of the need to

economize on energy use as prices rise as part of their continued cost

minimization strategy, though even here knowledge of foreign experience could accelerate the indicated adjustments. The response of households is more conjectural, since tastes, habits, and life-styles are involved, along with economic motivations. It is perhaps particularly here that international comparisons have some relevance, both as guides to workable policies and as warnings against unrealistic ones.

Theoretically, international comparisons can throw light on policy implementation as well as formulation. By observing the experience of other countries it might be possible to see which combination of price incentives and regulatory or institutional interventions seems most effective. Systematic reviews of international experiences can provide guidance on the relative effectiveness of alternative policy combinations and on pitfalls which may trap the unwary policy maker.

Most of the sectoral studies, while recognizing the importance of policy measures in determining energy consumption levels, have been unable to deal adequately with this topic because of lack of time. Authors of several studies, however, have indicated their intentions of following them up at a later date. In the meantime, Van Vactor of the International Energy Agency provided a comprehensive survey of IEA member countries' conservation policies in place.

In conclusion, although the workshop participants were in general agreement that international comparisons could offer useful insights on varying levels of energy consumption, they urged caution in how such comparisons were presented in terms of their utility for policy formulation and implemen- tation. In particular, they dismissed as oversimplistic and inaccurate the use of the aggregate energy/GDP ratio as a guide for policy, but felt that more disaggregated studies could provide useful information in this field where, thanks to historically cheap and abundant energy supplies in the past, little expertise exists.

This summary, in the interests of brevity, understates the differences in views which emerged at the workshop. But even here the division was sharper in concept than in practice. That is to say, those who felt that structural differences could be adequately quantified, yielding intensity differences which could be validly compared from one country to another, all urged extreme caution in using such intensity comparisons as firm guidelines for policy; while those who felt that structural characteristics were in practice very difficult to distinguish from intensity characteristics were willing to admit that such cases did exist and could illuminate differences in energy use.

Agenda for Research

Several directions for further research emerged from the workshop:

1. The need for work on a more extensive data base. As already explained, much of the existing international data on energy consumption and output measures has been exploited by the current crop of sectoral studies, and even these were considered deficient by some because of lack of data. Further work at more disaggregated levels of energy consumption will require more detailed data on industrial energy use, further detail on housing stock, a breakdown of passenger mileage into inter- and intracity categories, on input factor prices, capital stock vintage, and so on.

2. There appears good reason to press ahead with comparative international input-output studies once technical difficulties can be overcome. This approach more clearly distinguishes final demand uses from intermediate uses—a point felt to be of considerable analytic importance by many participants.

3. For the sectoral studies, particularly those dealing with a single year, there is an urgent need to extend the studies over a series of years. Some authors indicated their intention of doing this.

4. There is a great need for comparisons of policy instruments and their relative effectiveness. In particular, the role of energy prices--felt by all participants to be of major importance in determining levels of energy consumption--needs further investigation.

INTRODUCTORY REMARKS

Charles Hitch
Resources for the Future

Good morning. Welcome to the workshop. As you know, it is very much a
joint venture organized by Resources for the Future (RFF) with the financial
support of Electric Power Research Institute (EPRI). At the outset I want to
express to EPRI and particularly to its president, Dr. Chauncey Starr, our
great appreciation for this assistance.

Indeed, Chauncey Starr's involvement is a personal as well as a profes-
sional pleasure for me, for we have known each other for a number of years
now, going back to the late '60s and early '70s when we were both at the
University of California.

At the time Chauncey was a dean at UCLA and I was the systemwide
president, and the overall budget decisions I had to make eventually determined his levels of support. Although the situations are not exactly parallel,
the financial shoe is now on the other foot. Chauncey's decisions influence
whether RFF can do some things which we might otherwise not be able to afford.
The lesson is clear. Do unto others is far more than a religious concept.
Your next workshop could depend on it.

I should add that besides being an energetic instigator of the workshop,
Chauncey Starr is also a participant. He will be making a presentation of his
own work in the first panel of the day.

The events of today and tomorrow are part of a series of projects concerning international comparisons of energy consumption undertaken jointly by
EPRI and RFF. The first, entitled How Industrial Societies Use Energy, compares patterns of energy consumption in nine industrialized countries in 1972,
the last year of the old price order. You have already received a preprint

of the first and last chapters of this study. The complete study is now available. This work also will be presented in the first panel.

A second study is now getting under way to analyze energy consumption in some of these same countries over time. The purpose is to test the conclusions of the first study in a dynamic setting and also to extend the analysis to include comparisons of energy policies.

The joint interest of EPRI and RFF and indeed of all of you here in this field of international energy comparisons seems in retrospect to have been very prescient. Not so long ago when we were planning these projects, the extent of variations in energy consumption among otherwise comparable countries came as quite a surprise to many people, even to some who could be considered knowledgeable. Now this fact is not only widely known but it is rapidly becoming a standard oratorical gambit on the order of, "If we can put a man on the moon, then surely we can end crime or cure cancer or whatever."

Almost any speech on energy conservation these days quotes the example of countries which use less energy relative to output than we do. The President's national energy plan, for example, refers to the greater U.S. use of energy per dollar of gross national product compared with any other industrialized nation, and even devotes a whole page to a diagrammatic representation. We may be a little weary of comparisons with Sweden, but we can be gratified that a subject which started as a somewhat esoteric field of investigation is now being brought into the policymaking process.

The growing number of comparative studies and the way in which they are being used or misused in relation to policy matters seemed to us to offer a good opportunity for holding a workshop where those who have had extensive experience working in the field could meet and discuss their procedures and results. Further, we hope to find out what additional work is being done and what more needs to be done, and finally, we need to know what to make of it all, how to interpret our results, and what sort of conclusions can be drawn from them.

The organization of the workshop reflects these concerns. We start with a panel devoted to an overview of existing studies, followed by one on technical and methodological problems. I should like to emphasize that we have restricted this meeting solely to those with first-hand experience in the field. Though the subject has attracted the attention of a much wider circle, we felt that an open exchange of views could be better achieved in a small meeting composed of working specialists.

We did not wish to limit the workshop to results and technical aspects of international studies, but to move on and use international comparisons as a basis for discussing potentialities for energy conservation in this country in the three major energy-consuming sectors: buildings, transportation, and industry. The third panel will address these issues. Finally, in response to the current interest in energy policies, we have devoted a session to this topic.

This brings us to the final panel and the focus of our workshop: the uses and limitations of international energy consumption comparisons. I know enough of your writings to realize that there are considerable divergencies in your views about what can profitably be learned from the experience of other countries. I hope that they will serve only to sharpen our perception so that after sifting and winnowing we will part towmorrow afternoon having added to the body of knowledge about the intricate and still imperfectly understood relationship between energy needs and economic activity.

Thank you all very much for coming.

PART I

SURVEY OF EXISTING STUDIES

ENERGY USE: AN INTERREGIONAL ANALYSIS
WITH IMPLICATIONS FOR INTERNATIONAL COMPARISONS

Chauncey Starr
Electric Power Research Institute

The ratio of economic activity to total energy consumed in Btu's--the

Gross Domestic Product/energy ratio (GDP/E)--has been used extensively to

symbolize a relationship between an economic surrogate for the so-called

"well being" of societies and the consumption of energy inputs. Studies have

been conducted by Schurr et al. [18], Darmstadter et al. [7, 8], Schipper

and Lichtenberg [17], Goen and White [9], Netschert [13], Boretsky et al. [5],

and Berndt and Wood [1, 2], to name a few authors. This GDP/E ratio has been

hailed by the popular press as a measure of the efficiency with which nations

use energy fuels. More, the comparisons with foreign countries have been

used to indicate the potential for energy conservation in the United States.

For example, in a recent Business Week article [22] it was pointed out

that West Germany's industrial sector uses 38 percent less energy per unit of

output than American industry: Sweden uses 40 percent less energy to pro-

duce each dollar of GDP. On the consumption side, this article stated that

Swedish homes burn less fuel than American homes, and that Swedish cars get

24 miles per gallon: and the Swedish drive less because they have an

excellent transportation system. Aside from the uncertain validity of these

numbers, the implication is that based on the example of these countries,

achieving conservation savings in the United States of 30-40 percent should

be readily possible. Such international lists of "they use energy better

than us" suggests to readers that the United States is sloppy in its use of

energy.

The merit of these contentions depends on the interpretation of the

meaning and significance of GDP/E ratios. That is, what information does the

GDP/E ratio provide? Can GDP/E comparisons measure the relative "efficiency" of energy use? And based on these relative measures, is there some information that would tell us how, or in what way, we should redirect our resources to better uses? Allied to all of this, can such ratios aid us in making projections for future energy planning? It is to these questions that this paper is addressed.

Problems in Measuring Economic Efficiency

In mechanics, work output divided by energy input is defined as a measure of efficiency, and the higher the efficiency of a system, the closer efficiency is to unity. We all know this. But the world of economics is not the world of theoretical or applied mechanics. As is demonstrated below, GDP divided by energy does not measure how efficient the United States, or some other society, is in its use of energy. In the generation of some GDP, energy is only one factor of production. Capital, labor, and materials are also factor inputs. And societies (industries and firms) combine these factors in different ways to produce outputs. Just what combinations evolve depends on several factors, one of which is prices. If one society shows a high GDP/E ratio relative to another, this does not mean that some given society is more efficient in its energy use. Certainly, there are alternative interpretations, e.g., that the allocation of factor inputs is different for each country. Their resource base, technology, industrial mix, and so on are different. Or should the price of energy be relatively high, one country may substitute labor for energy; another, capital for energy.[1] This is not to say that GDP/E is not a useful parameter in energy analysis. In any given region, with only slowly changing factors of production, this ratio does permit useful trend

---

[1]Griffin and Gregory [10], employing international cross-sectional data, suggest that, in the long-run, capital and labor are substitutable for energy.

analysis and can provide insight to the regional energy use patterns.

To illustrate the inadequacies of using GDP/E ratios to measure the relative "efficiencies" of countries, table 1 provides a combination list of alternative economic measures. For example, economic value could be combined in ratio form with capital, labor, energy, materials, or technology: alternatively, physical output could be combined with any one of the resource variables, and so on. The ratios generated would likely be different for each country, but no conclusions could be drawn as to the relative "efficiencies" of capital, labor, energy, materials, or technology employment from such ratios. In fact, such ratios omit the key elements of the existing industrial infrastructure and the organization and management of productive units.

If the goal is to measure "economic efficiency", then one approach is to define efficiency as the ratio,

$$\frac{\text{Actual economic output}}{\text{Maximum economic output}}$$

for a given mix of resources. Here a ratio of unity defines optimum efficiency and is achieved when the value of each (marginal) productive services equals its alternative cost.[2] Obviously, if the alternative cost is less than the value of the marginal product, a unit of the productive service will produce more in this use than elsewhere, and output is not at a maximum. If the alternative cost exceeds the value of the marginal product in any use, a unit of the productive service will produce more elsewhere, and output is not at a maximum. Optimum efficiency, a ratio of unity, is achieved when the value of the marginal product of each productive service equals its alternative cost. A difference between alternative cost and the value of the marginal product (say, for energy) in any firm or industry is proof of inefficiency, and the magnitude of the difference is a clue to the extent of the inefficiency.

---

[2]Alternative (or opportunity) cost is the maximum amount that any productive service would produce in any commodity. [20]

TABLE 1

ALTERNATIVE ECONOMIC MEASURES

GOODS & SERVICES		RESOURCES
Physical output		Capital
Economic value	VS	Labor
Physical consumption		Energy
Utility		Materials
		Technology

We suspect that the condition for maximum output (measured in terms of the prices consumers are willing to pay) is being fulfilled in free market Western societies today. That is, energy is being employed up to the point where its marginal product just equals its alternative cost. If this is the case, then Sweden, West Germany and the United States have equal economic efficiency in their use of energy.

Interregional Comparisons

Another tack to providing insight into the problems of using GDP/E ratios for comparative purposes, is to make an interregional analysis. This we have done in our "Proficiency" paper [19] where we have given a look at the differences in economic output and energy use in each state of the United States. What did we learn from this exercise?

As expected, we found a wide range of energy use and aggregate economic levels between the states of the United States, explained in part, by differences in the mix of economic activities and from the differences in energy consumption per unit output of these activities. Each state has its own economic characteristics which has evolved from its location, natural resource base, population (and concomitant labor force), and other parameters. But more, each state has developed and grown as part of the whole United States economic structure, a structure based on the relatively free flow of resources (including energy), labor, materials, semi-finished and finished goods between states. That is, through the division of economic activities (or specialization), the benefits from interstate trade have become large for society as a whole.

Figure 1 discloses the wide range of energy use and economic activity that existed between the states in 1971. However, to argue and compare the efficiency of states by their respective Gross State Product (GSP)/E ratios does not mean one state is more energy efficient than another. On the contrary, each state is engaged in economic activities associated with

FIGURE 1

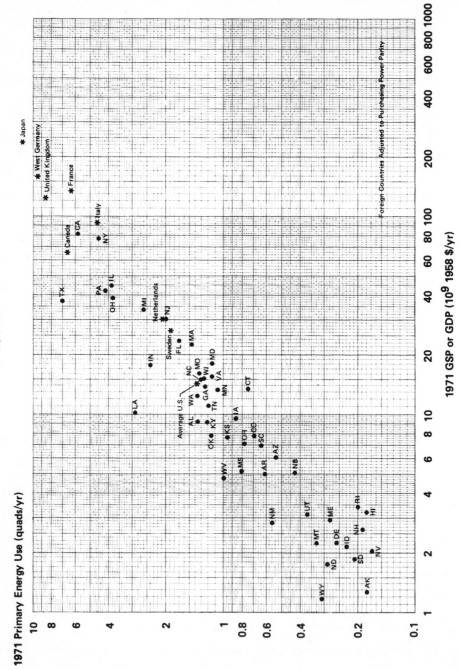

GROSS PRODUCT VS ENERGY USE
1971

different energy requirements. Compare, e.g., Wyoming and Vermont,Vermont and Louisiana, or Texas with New Jersey. A cross-sectional sample of state data points for 1971 is provided in table 2 below. Both Wyoming and Vermont have similar Gross State Products, but Vermont uses far less energy than Wyoming. The GSP/E ratios tell us so. Is Vermont more energy efficient than Wyoming, than Lousiana or Texas?

The corollary between states and inter-country comparisons is an interesting one in that GDP/E comparisons are just as involved as they are for states. Can we compare Sweden, West Germany, or Japan with the United States using GDP/E ratios? Perhaps a more likely comparison would be between Florida and Sweden; the Netherlands with New Jersey; Italy with New York; Canada with California. None of the comparisons, of course, are really justified using economic/energy ratios. Each country is as different as each state, and there is a certain absurdity in trying to compare energy use in one to another; to conclude one is more energy efficient than another.

Issues in International Comparisons

We have all seen, in the publications cited, comparative international GDP/E tables or plots, where GDP in foreign currencies is converted to U.S. dollars using exchange rates, or the more meaningful purchasing power parity indexes [12], and deflated to constant dollars. Additionally, energy and national output may be on a per capita basis. Sweden, the Netherlands, West Germany, the United Kingdom, France, Italy, and Japan, to name a few countries, all have higher ratios than the United States. And it is assumed, or explicitly stated, that these countries use energy more "efficiently" than the United States. As have been pointed out, this, of course, is misleading. But more, there are a number of issues that need to be raised from this type of analysis; questions of whether or not such analysis holds any constructive meaning for the United States.

TABLE 2

SAMPLE DATA: STATE PAIRS, 1971

	Wyoming	Vermont	Louisiana	Connecticut	Texas	New Jersey
*GSP 1971 ($ Billions/Yr.)	1.3	1.5	10.9	14.3	40.4	31.2
Energy Use (quads**/Yr.)	0.33	0.084	3.07	0.78	7.55	1.98
GSP/E ($ million Btu)	3.9	17.5	3.6	18.4	5.4	15.8

*GSP = $\dfrac{\text{State personal income}}{\text{National personal income}}$ X GDP.   Methodology from (11).

**quad = 10^{15} Btu

Production vs. Consumption

At issue, there appears to be some confusion in the literature as to what is being measured: the production of goods and services and the relative "efficiency" of energy input to the creation of any given GDP bundle, or the relative consumption of goods and services and the energy bedded therein. That is, energy use in any given economy occurs mainly in those intermediate activities that produce goods and services that are measured by GDP.   The remainder of the energy (whose price is included in GDP) is used to satisfy final demand, i.e., purchases by final consumers for such things as home heating fuels, residential electricity, gasoline, and so on.   Obviously, the split between energy for final demand and for economic output is implicit in the GDP/E ratios.   For example, from table 3, in 1972, total primary energy used in the United States was 72.9 quads.   Of this 45.2 quads or 62 percent of the total were employed in the intermediate production process.   27.7 quads were consumed as final demand.   This split, of course, is important, and the breakdown of how energy is being consumed in the final demand category, and the various allocations being made in the industrial production sectors need to be identified.   And they will vary from society to society. But simple GDP/E ratios do not tell us this, and if the intent is to identify the relationship between energy use and output, (the "efficiencies" of energy to the creation of some level of GDP) then we are talking about production. Here the mix of industry, technology, price, resources, and so on need to be considered.   Alternatively, if the final consumption side of energy is to be considered, besides price and income, the mix of goods and services available and their energy intensities, demographic characteristics, lifestyles, climate, and so on will need to be reviewed.   Confusing the two can result in incorrect interpretations.

Allied to the issue of production vs. consumption is the question of

TABLE 3

PRIMARY ENERGY USE IN THE U.S. 1972
10^{15} Btu/yr

	ECONOMIC OUTPUT ACTIVITIES	FINAL DEMAND	TOTAL PRIMARY ENERGY
Coal	12.2	2.2 (including 1.8 exported)	14.4
Oil	15.4	18.2	33.6
Gas	15.3	6.1	21.4
Hydroelectric	1.9	1.0	2.9
Nuclear	0.4	0.2	0.6
TOTAL	45.2	27.7	72.9

embodied energy, i.e., whether or not the final consumers of a product should be charged for its embodied energy (i.e., all the energy inputs required for its production), or whether that society (or state) which receives the value added in the production process should be charged directly for the energy it employs. It would appear that if one is focusing on production, or the relationship in each country between the economic value generated (GDP) and the energy required to create this economic value, that it makes little economic sense for the energy embodied in final product to be charged to the country that consumes the final product. That is, energy, in some combination with capital, labor, and materials was employed to help generate some level of GDP, effective demand, and employment. Thus, the employment of Btu's contributes to the so called "well being" of any society. And in the I/O relationship of GDP/E, subtracting out the energy employed for products exported obviously incorrectly biases the ratio upwards. Similarly, adding embodied energy in imports, incorrectly biases the ratio downward. In comparative analysis, such interpretation would be misleading if the objective is to compare "efficiencies" or "effectiveness" of energy usage to the economic values generated.

But, if one is asking the question of how much energy is a nation consuming, not in terms of production, but in terms of world wide contributions of energy to consumption, then embodied energy may be considered pertinent. But the intentions of such analysis must be clearly stated; namely, to show the additional amounts of energy consumed from traded goods. But then, comparative analysis, and any presumption from this analysis, that concludes that foreign practices and consumption would be profitable to explore would be misleading if "efficiencies" or "effectiveness" is the intent. That is, the analysis would be in terms of consumption patterns, and not the productivity of of energy use.

An extremely simple example illustrating the consumption/production

18

FIGURE 2

EMBODIED ENERGY
Consumption/Production Viewpoint

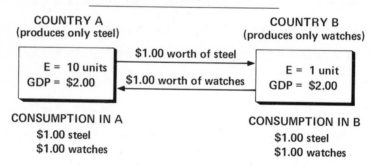

ASSUMPTIONS

- Equal economic output
- Equal consumption patterns
- Different production patterns
- Balanced trade

COUNTRY A
(produces only steel)

COUNTRY B
(produces only watches)

E = 10 units
GDP = $2.00

$1.00 worth of steel

$1.00 worth of watches

E = 1 unit
GDP = $2.00

CONSUMPTION IN A
$1.00 steel
$1.00 watches

CONSUMPTION IN B
$1.00 steel
$1.00 watches

viewpoint is provided in figure 2. Here countries A and B each consume one dollar worth of steel and one dollar worth of watches. The energy intensity of steel is 5 units of energy per dollar; the intensity of watches, .5 units of energy per dollar. It is assumed that the import by country B of one dollar's worth of steel is equivalent to the import of five units of energy. Similarly, import of one dollar's worth of watches by country A is equivalent to the import of .5 units of energy.

Using the production viewpoint with this example, the GDP/energy ratios when not adjusted for imports and exports are 0.2 for country A, and 2 for country B. The philosophy behind this is contained in the question: How much output (GDP) does a country produce with a given amount of energy? When adjustments are made for imported embodied energy, the GDP/energy ratio of 0.36 is the same for both country A and B. If the consumption viewpoint is employed both countries look equally energy consuming, alternatively, given the production viewpoint, country B would appear more energy "efficient" than country A. Neither approach serves to tell us whether one country is more or less "economic efficient" than the other.

Industry Mix

Another issue is that of industry mix. In our "Proficiency" paper, we noted the tremendous variations in value added and energy use for some 87 sectors in the United States' economy [21]. And it was shown that heavy industries such as iron, steel manufacturing, chemicals, oil and gas extraction, petroleum refining and paper require substantially more energy for a specific level of value added than other economic activities such as printing and publishing, finance, and insurance. Figure 3 provides a broad brush picture of the economic activities in the United States for the year 1972. And those states such as Texas and Louisiana that are noted for a large proportion of energy-intensive industries, e.g., petroleum refining and petrochemicals,

FIGURE 3

ECONOMIC ACTIVITIES IN THE U.S.
1972

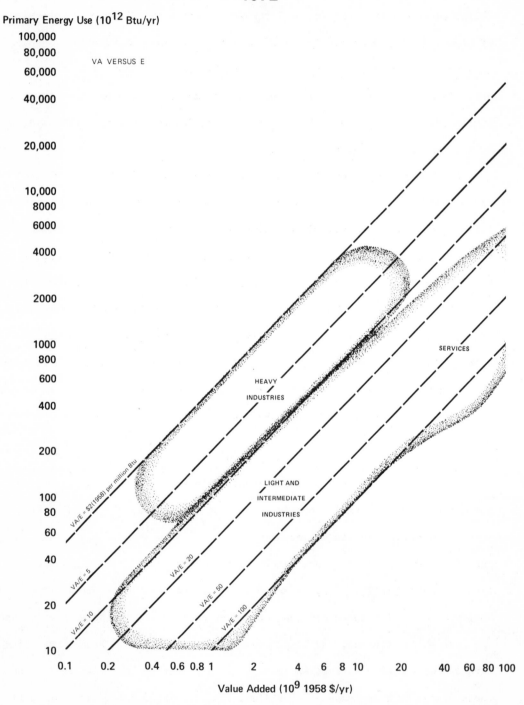

Primary Energy Use (10^{12} Btu/yr)

Value Added (10^9 1958 $/yr)

and Indiana, Ohio, and Pennsylvania where steel manufacturing is prominent, all have much lower GSP/E ratios than those states that provide services such as New York which specializes in banking, insurance, and real estate.

Another interesting feature is shown in figure 4 in that those states that have a relatively low GSP/E ratio are predominately energy exporters. Most of these energy source states not only have installed energy-intensive conversion facilities such as oil and gas extraction plants, but energy-intensive satellite industries have located and developed in nearby areas. Similarly, in looking at the GDP/E ratio internationally versus the dependence on energy imports, figure 5 for selected countries [8], shows a similar relationship.

This relationship between the GDP/E ratio and dependence on energy imports is an interesting one in that higher ratios appear to be associated with greater energy dependence. Part of the explanation lies in the fact that those societies that have become increasingly dependent on energy imports have orchestrated policy directed to minimize this dependence, e.g., tax policies directed to raise energy price levels, particularly on petroleum products. These higher prices not only restrict the quantities being consumed, but act as a mechanism to allocate energy to more efficient uses. And, in part, these higher prices will serve to shift the industrial base away from energy-intensive type industries to less energy-intensive types, or from those industries with low value added contributions to high valued added sectors.

The point is that the industrial mix for each society is likely to be different, and because of these differences, the quantities of energy employed for production will be different. And if comparable data could be found for the major western societies, the differences in industrial mix would become clearer, and help to explain variations in energy use.

Additionally, comparisons of aggregate data for specific industries can

FIGURE 4

GSP/E or GDP/E VS E/L FOR U.S. & FOREIGN COUNTRIES 1971

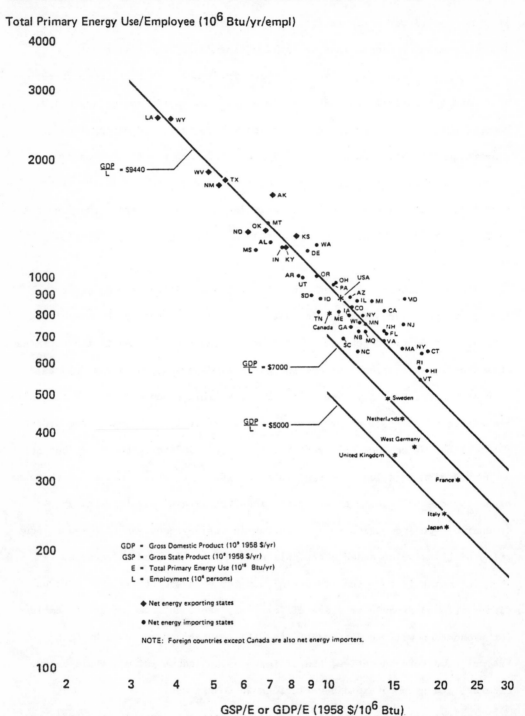

Total Primary Energy Use/Employee (10^6 Btu/yr/empl)

FIGURE 5

GDP/E VS DEPENDENCE ON ENERGY IMPORTS FOR 1972

GDP/E (1958 $/$10^6$ Btu)

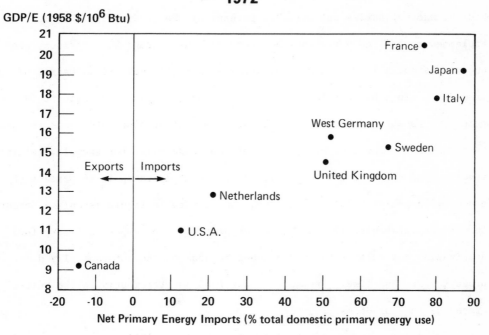

Net Primary Energy Imports (% total domestic primary energy use)

be misleading. As examples, we can point to two major industries; petroleum refining and steelmaking. The summary of the SRI report [9] indicates that West German energy use is 67 percent of that of the United States per ton of petroleum products manufactured. That is to say that the average United States refinery uses 11.2 percent of the crude oil as refinery fuel; whereas, West German refineries use only 7.5 percent of the crude oil. This is explained to a large degree by the fact that the average U.S. refinery produces substantially more gasoline, kerosene and jet fuel from a barrel of crude oil. To achieve this greater production of light products, it is necessary to use fuel to provide the process heat necessary to crack the heavy hydrocarbons in the fuel oil portion of the crude oil. For example, catalytic cracking and hydro cracking capacity in the United States is 36 percent of crude oil capacity. In West Germany, the comparable figure is only 4 percent. On a first cut basis, it would seem inappropriate to compare refinery fuel utilization per unit of refined product because of the substantially different product mix. And likely, refineries use fuel as efficiently in the United States as in West Germany.

Concerning steel manufacturing, after mining, milling and concentration, iron ore is sent to a blast furnace which derives most of its heat from the energy in the coke that is added. The energy requirement in the United States in 1972 was about 42.6 MM Btu/short ton of pig iron. Ore concentrations in the United States are about 50-55 percent iron; whereas, in Sweden, ores are richer in iron [60-65 percent Fe]. The richer ore probably has less requirement for energy. Thereafter, pig iron is mixed with scrap steel (derived from both outside purchase and internal mill recycling) and sent to three types of secondary processing: basic oxygen, open hearth, and electric furnace, the product of which is raw steel. The choice of secondary processing is dependent not only on economics but also on the type of steel

to be made. Sweden has the reputation of being the "jeweler" of the steel
industry. That is, they produce, on the average, a higher value added
product. This is reflected in figures from Schipper [17].

Value Added/Primary Energy
(1971 $/MM Btu)

	United States	Sweden
Basic steel	3.4	6.8
Primary metals (incl. basic steel)	4.5	5.3

But these figures do not reflect feedstock variations, processing variations and differing product mixes and certainly they do not allow one to
estimate conservation potential.

The point of all this is that as one subdivides the aggregate figures
for each industry, it becomes clear that each industrial sector is quite
complex and quick conclusions are not attainable. It is necessary to examine
in detail feedstock quality, product mix and specifications and the use of
recycle materials all in relationship to current and anticipated costs of
capital, labor, energy, and materials in order to understand international
differences.

Lifestyles

Another important issue when comparing GDP/E ratios is that of lifestyles.
Here, of course, we are referring to the consumption side of GDP, and not the
generation of product. Certainly, the way we live, our "habits" of consumption can be of importance when the conservation of energy becomes an issue.

In the United States itself, the South has much lower incomes than the
Northeast and the West Coast. States such as Mississippi have scarcely
attained per capita incomes equal to those reached in Pennsylvania and

New York in 1925 or those found in France today. In other words, per capita incomes vary from state to state. But per capita incomes (and even the prices of energy) may not sufficiently serve for us to understand why there are differing consumption patterns of energy. In addition, social, political, other economic, and environmental conditions also vary from state to state, or from region to region, i.e., lifestyles, or indexes of "the quality of life" may help in interpreting, and explaining differences in energy consumption. And these lifestyles, the social environment in which people live, should be subject to analysis in international energy comparison studies.

Two recent studies by the Midwest Research Institute [3, 4] show that the quality of life varies from state to state and from Standard Metropolitan Statistical Area to Standard Metropolitan Statistical Area (SMSA). Based on a composite index of social, economic, political, and environmental variables, California ranked number 1, Colorado #2, Alabama #50. On an income per capita basis, California ranked #5, Colorado #21, and Alabama #44. In other words, income per capita may not serve as a sufficient measure to explain the "well being" of people, and the overall environment in which they live. For an overall index for large SMSA's, Portland, Oregon ranked #1; Jersey City, New Jersey #65.

Based on these differences in lifestyles or the qualities of life in the United States, we would expect to find differences on an international basis. One international study [16] supports this contention. In this study a composite index was developed that included, e.g., the number of telephones, cars, radios, and television sets in use; the share of expenditures for food, drink, clothing, rent, recreation and energy in personal consumption, and so on, for Holland, Luxemburg, Belgium, West Germany, Austria, and Italy, all measures to quantify lifestyles in these EEC countries. Not surprising, wide differences in lifestyles were supported by this historical evidence, i.e.,

FIGURE 6

PATH OF ENERGY USE

PROCESS	*FACTORS*
Resource Extraction & Transportation	Quality Method Location Relative to Markets
Conversion to Secondary Form	Feed Mix Output Mix (demand) Externalities (vis environment) Method
Distribution	Demography Externalities (vis remote siting)
Conversion to Work-end Function	Mechanical Efficiency Capital Stock Energy Component Input Mix Quality Performance Requirements

the people in Holland have different lifestyles from those in Italy, or
Austria.

A more recent publication [6] shows the relationship between man's use
of energy and the social fabric or lifestyles of that society for different
countries of the world; again, pointing out that people do live differently
and employ energy in uses based on that lifestyle. Additionally, Cook points
out changes in lifestyles are partially brought about through increased uses
of energy, i.e., there is a positive relation between energy and the way
people live.

The point is that in looking at and comparing energy use in societies,
lifestyles are an important parameter, too often neglected in analytical
efforts. And what is required in international energy comparative studies
is to give a hard look at how people live, because energy consumption is
going to be reflected in any given societies' lifestyle. The task is not an
easy one as the quality of life or lifestyles mean different things to different people, and, at present, no consensus exists as to what it is or what it
means. Yet a consensus does exist regarding its importance as related to
energy, and for this reason it needs to be explored further. And in its
exploration, international differences in energy consumption may become
clearer.

Maximizing End Function and Minimizing Resource Utilization

Interregional comparisons have two useful onjectives. The most important is their continuing contribution to understanding energy flow and human
welfare. A second objective is based on the hope that such studies will
disclose regional conservation potential from available aggregate measures.
For reasons stated above, this is not possible.

As figure 6 shows, the efficiency of energy use (defined by the relative
primary fuel requirement to produce a given end function) is the product of

a chain of individual process efficiencies. In each process of the resource-to-end function sequence, external factors do play a role. When these external factors are significantly different among countries, the use of international data on a sector basis is misleading.

Examples of some end functions are environmental conditioning (heating, air conditioning, lighting), transportation, labor savings (as through appliances), recreation, and health maintenance (as through refrigeration, cooking, clothes washing and drying, and most domestic hot water uses). In intermediate processes, energy is used for physical or chemical separation or joining of materials, the gathering of materials (such as mining or harvesting), transportation of materials, and delivery of most of the final demand services listed above.

The external factors which affect the efficiency of each stage of the energy use process (see figure 6) are, in some cases, included in published international comparisons. An example of such a factor is climate; a correction for degree-days in a heating comparison is typically made. Other external factors, usually omitted, include differing socially imposed externalities such as environmental requirements, quality differences such as time (the time savings of air travel versus bus transportation), and comfort and safety (small cars versus large cars).

In summary, quality differences exist among the processes and end functions, as in differences in refinery or steel mill product mix, or in the convenience differences between automobiles and mass transit. It is only after these quality differences have been recognized, and their contribution to energy demand analyzed, that comparisons of this sort can indicate areas likely to yield significant energy savings.

An example of such a comparison is shown in figure 7 [15]. This comparison, between a gasoline powered and electric powered car, assumes vehicles

FIGURE 7

SYSTEM EFFICIENCY
Gas vs Electric Car Federal Driving Cycle

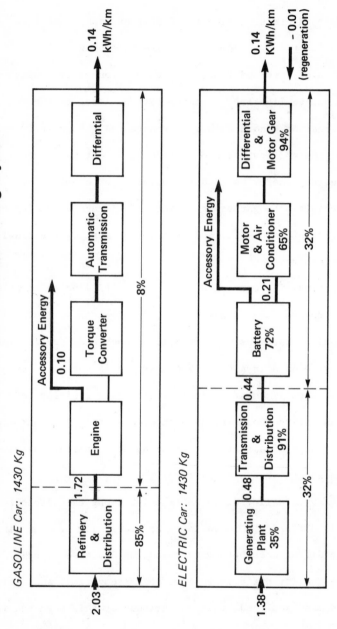

FIGURE 8

TECHNICAL & LIFE STYLE CONSERVATION

TECHNICAL

- Improvement in Process Efficiency
- Process Substitution for Same End Function

LIFE STYLE

- Change End Function Mix
- Change End Function Quality
- Reduce Externality Constraints

of identical weight, presumed to offer equivalent utility. Comparisons between total systems such as these do indicate a measure of the resource consumption for a specific end function.

This example (figure 7) illustrates the second path to conservation as indicated on figure 8--a process change. In this same vein, a conversion to diesel would provide improvements in individual process efficiencies (as diesels are more efficient than gasoline engines and refineries use less energy in the production of diesel oil than of gasoline), as well as represent a process change.

The comparison and examination on a case by case basis of the primary energy flow pattern in the system used to perform various end functions will serve to direct conservation efforts better than will the comparison of more aggregated data. Such an examination can indicate the relative importance of process efficiencies, sequences of processes, or quality changes in end functions.

Quality of Energy Resources

One feature of interregional comparisons on a "per Btu" basis that limits their value to a national planning effort is the usual failure to discriminate between the relative performance of different fuels. While this is not a novel point (Boretsky has used weighting factors for various fuels), it needs to be addressed in these international comparisons [5].

In the United States today, we are developing methods to convert coal to clean liquid and gaseous fuels with "Btu" efficiencies of between 50 percent and 80 percent. The large scale implementation of these systems would obviously increase gross energy consumption relative to the Btu content of the oil and gas, but given the large coal resources of the United States such systems may be acceptable. Currently, coal and uranium are usable on a large scale only after conversion to electricity, and the necessary heat rejection during conversion is frequently mentioned as proof of the "inherent inefficiency" of electricity. While it is clear that, on a per Btu basis, the use of electricity for space heating requires more primary energy than the direct consumption of natural gas, it is not clear that the latter method is preferable if other than Btu comparisons are made. Figure 9 evaluates a number of heating strategies by the amount of oil and gas consumed [14]. In this figure, the oil and gas consumption for electric heating is based on their fraction of the total primary fuel used for electricity nationally. While this measure is too simple for general application, it does point out the value of alternative viewpoints as to what should be conserved, as well as how much. For example, if the objective is reduction in oil and gas use, and coal and uranium are unrestricted, electricity for space heating would be chosen.

The Btu measure of fuel value is appropriate for processes which lead to low temperature heating, which represents the lowest valued use of fuel. Comparisons of primary energy use for other types of conversion, such as from potential energy to mechanical motion, high temperature heat, or light are poorly served by this measure.

Even for applications with heat as an end function, this simple calorimetric comparison ignores the overall sequence efficiency of use for most applications. As an example, the energy potential of a high mountain lake can be converted to electricity with 90 percent efficiency, delivered with 91 percent efficiency, and used to generate heat with 100 percent efficiency (or more if a heat pump is used). This 82 percent system efficiency is substantially higher than the efficiencies found in any fossil fuel system. As a result, most energy analysts have adopted a quality multiplier for hydroelectric energy to put it on the same basis as fossil fuel electricity. While such a multiplier seems appropriate, it seems that other multipliers for other fuels would be equally appropriate.

FIGURE 9

OIL & GAS CONSUMPTION FOR
FUTURE HEATING SCENARIOS

Residential Scarce-Fuel Use (10^{12} Btu/yr)

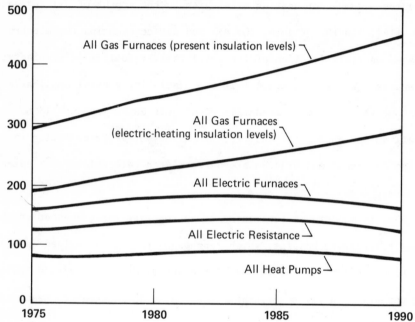

The concept of weighting factors for different fuels leads immediately to inconsistencies. As an example, the energy value of oil relative to coal for electricity generation is roughly equivalent on a Btu basis, because the system efficiencies are about the same. The system efficiency of oil is much higher than that of coal if a comparison of transportation applications (diesel vs. steam) is made, and its use should be weighted accordingly. While it is theoretically possible to weight the value of each fuel by a factor which reflects the aggregate of end use functions to which it is applied, such a factor would be inappropriate for specific end use comparisons.

The issue of resource quality is handled quite nicely by market economics when given a chance. It seems likely that the aggregate weighting functions for various fuels could be inferred from their free market prices. If this is true, then on a basis of social value per Btu, hydroelectric potential is more valuable than natural gas, gas more valuable than oil, oil more than coal, coal more than uranium, and uranium more valuable than sunlight. A wise conservation policy is one which recognizes these quality differences and does not measure success simply by the number of Btu's saved.

Conclusions

In the introduction, a number of international comparison studies were cited. The question, of course, is what are the implications of these studies? Do they provide us with guidelines, or alternative ways of using energy? Not in their present state of analysis. What they have shown is that for some comparable total bundle of goods and services energy used in a number of European countries is less than in the United States. But part is due to the inter-industry mix, part to lifestyles, differences in prices of factor inputs, the prices of final products, incomes, climate, geography, natural resource base, technology, and so on. The list is, indeed, formidable. But this list does suggest the complexities involved when trying to compare energy use in different societies. In other words, GDP/E ratios can be expected to be different in each country, reflecting the most efficient way to do things for that society. How they do things, how they combine their resources, how they use their energy does not mean that their way is the way we should follow. Is it not possible, should the United States emulate any country, or combination of countries, that the misallocations of our resources could be large? Rather than emulate any country, market forces (prices) will do a lot towards adjusting and reallocating energy to its best use with conservation taking place in the process. The United States economic system, its society, is capable of making change, adjusting to the new (higher) prices of energy. History has shown us again and again of this flexible capability.

To sum up: the problem of comparing countries and their respective energy uses is a complex one, and simple GDP/E ratio comparisons can lead to the wrong conclusions. Let us avoid that. Certainly, such ratios do not measure efficiency. Hopefully, our state comparisons will provide some insights into the complexity of the issues involved, and why there are differences in energy use.

References

1. E. Berndt and D. Wood, "An Economic Interpretation of the Energy-GNP
    Ratio" in M. Macrakis, (ed.) Energy: Demand, Conservation, and
    Institutional Problems, Cambridge, MIT Press, Chapt. 3, 1974.

2. E. Berndt and D. Wood, "Technology, Prices, and the Derived Demand
    for Energy," Review of Economic Statistics, August, 1975.

3. B-C Liu, "Quality of Life in the United States, 1970"
    (Midwest Research Institute, Kansas City, Mo., 1975).

4. B-C Liu, "Quality of Life in the U.S. Metropolitan Areas, 1970"
    (Midwest Research Institute, Kansas City, Mo., 1975).

5. M. Boretsky, et al., "Potentialities and Limitations for Conservation
    in the United States Apparent in Differential Uses of Energy Abroad,"
    (Office of Policy Development, Office of the Secretary, Washington,
    D.C., Revised Draft, 1975).

6. E. Cook, Man, Energy, Society, San Francisco, W.H. Freeman & Co., 1976.

7. J. Darmstadter, et al., Energy in the World Economy, Resources for
    the Future, Baltimore, The Johns Hopkins Univ. Press, 1971.

8. J. Darmstadter, J. Dunkerley, J. Alterman, How Industrial Societies
    Use Energy: A Comparative Analysis, Baltimore, Johns Hopkins University
    Press for Resources for the Future, 1977.

9. R. Goen and R. White, "Comparison of Energy Consumption Between
    West Germany and the United States," (Stanford Research Institute,
    Palo Alto, Ca., 1975).

10. J. Griffin and P. Gregory, "An Intercountry Translog Model of Energy
    Substitution Responses," The American Economic Review, Dec. 1976.

11. J. Kendrick and C. Jaycox, "The Concept and Estimation of Gross
    State Product", The Southern Economic Journal, Oct. 1965, Vol. 32.

12. I. Kravis, et al, A System of International Comparisons of Gross
    Product and Purchasing Power, Baltimore, The Johns Hopkins Univ.
    Press, 1975.

13. B. Netschert, "Fuels for the Electric Utility Industry, 1971-1985,"
    (National Economic Research Associates, Washington, D.C., 1972).

14. J. Oplinger, "Electric heating can save scarce fuels", Electric
    World, October 15, 1975.

15. J. Salihi, "Kilowatthours vs. Liters", IEEE Spectrum, March 1975.

16. L. Scheer, "The Quality of Life: A Try at a European Comparison,"
    in EPA, The Quality of Life Concept a Potential New Tool for Decision-
    Makers, Washington, D.C., U.S. Government Printing Office, 1973.

References (continued)

17. L. Schipper and A. Lichtenberg, "Efficient Energy Use and Well-Being: The Swedish Example," Science, Dec. 1976.

18. S. Schurr, et al., Energy in the American Economy, 1850-1955: An Economic Analysis of its History and Prospects, Baltimore, The Johns Hopkins Univ. Press, 1960.

19. C. Starr and S. Field, "Energy Use Proficiency: The Validity of Interregional Comparisons," (Electric Power Research Institute, Palo Alto, Ca., 1977).

20. G. Stigler, The Theory of Price, New York, The Macmillan Co., 1952.

21. U.C., Lawrence Berkeley Laboratory, A Linear Economic Model of Fuel and Energy Use in the United States (A report to EPRI - ES-115, Dec. 1975).

22 "Will Energy Conservation Throttle Economic Growth?" Business Week, (April 25, 1977, pp. 66-80).

A SECTIONAL ANALYSIS OF INTERNATIONAL ENERGY CONSUMPTION PATTERNS: SUMMARY

Scott Johnson
The Open University (U.K.)

Disaggregated sectoral analyses are necessary to arrive at significant intercountry measures of energy consumption relative to GDP. All such comparisons must distinguish between structural differences in countries' energy consumption patterns and differences in energy intensiveness. Future changes in consumption patterns will reflect not only inherent structural factors but also technically feasible energy conservation possibilities, and the dynamic of the cultural, economic, and political realities of a country.

Several countries were compared to determine if large differences in sector size accounted for intercountry variations in energy consumption. Within Western Europe, it was apparent that substantial differences did not exist, nor did any one sector dominate primary energy consumption. The percentage of GDP arising from the less energy intensive service sector appears to be increasing at the expense of the manufacturing sector. This trend exemplifies the importance of the structure of GDP and its relation to aggregate energy consumption.

The mix of primary fuels in final consumption plays a large role in determining energy consumption in the energy industries. The problem of assigning a comparable heat content is particularly troublesome for hydro and nuclear electricity. These two are usually measured on a primary energy equivalents basis, but this leaves some doubt as to the validity of comparison for countries with a large hydro resource. The primary fuel mix may also reflect the security of supply, especially in countries with a large import dependence. The relatively low conversion efficiency of fossil fuels to electricity isolates electricity generation as a particularly sensitive area. There is substantial variation between countries in the amount of fossil fuels converted to electricity and, in addition, variation in the efficiency with which the electricity is generated. Together, this would suggest that many possibilities exist to learn about energy conservation. However, vested interests and political pressures militate against such change. Further, although countries characterized by high conversion losses would, in theory, be expected to achieve efficient final uses for the electricity, in practice there is little relationship between conversion and final fuels both relative to GDP.

In the industry sector, high levels of disaggregation are necessary to compare energy intensities in particular industries. Several factors of comparability must be introduced as a requirement of valid analysis, such as homogeneous measures of both input and output, and similarity of the industrial process.

Expectations concerning future shortages and supplies are key factors determining investment in energy conservation. Increased import dependence will likely motivate industry to use less energy-intensive processes. Thus, the oil embargo of 73/74 and speculation on future shortages can be expected to have a continuing effect of reducing energy consumption in industry. The path of economic growth will also influence the pace of investment in energy conservation equipment.

Transport contributes the smallest amount to the total energy consumed, but presents some notable opportunities for energy savings. Not surprisingly, the bus is more efficient than the automobile in terms of energy consumption/

passenger mile; rail is superior to road transport in energy consumption/ freight mile; and air transport for both passengers and freight is the least efficient. The small variation in passenger road transport between the countries considered here (mainly Europe) and the large variations in freight suggest large differences in load factors. Significant energy savings will require vigorous policy changes to change the structure of transport.

The domestic, commercial, and agricultural sectors are generally grouped under one heading, but the focus for energy savings is on fuel use in buildings. Variation in consumption patterns is partially attributable to climatic differences, but also includes the temperature maintained in buildings, the size of buildings, and the standard of insulation adopted in a country. The most significant factors contributing to intercountry differences are the insulation standards, the use of electrical resistive heating, and the use of combined heat and power generation.

In conclusion, the sectoral analysis of energy consumption in developed countries shows:

(1) Intercountry differences in energy consumption patterns exist that can not be adequately explained with reference to a single index of welfare such as GDP.

(2) Different factors contributing toward energy consumption are important in different countries. Speculation on future trends is meaningful only with the consideration of an individual country's experience.

(3) Substantial opportunities to conserve exist in all countries and all sectors, in various amounts, and without directly affecting output.

There is the possibility that to achieve some degree of energy conservation, a change in lifestyles may be necessary. The role of government must also be considered: it may have other, contradictory objectives with respect to prices, employment, growth, and balance of payments. Moreover, to effect significant changes, government may be required to directly intervene in new areas.

INTERCOUNTRY COMPARISONS OF ENERGY USE - FINDINGS
FROM A RECENTLY COMPLETED RFF REPORT: SUMMARY

Joel Darmstadter
Resources for the Future

Discussions of energy-conservation potentials in the United States have frequently taken note of the lower levels of per capita energy consumption prevailing in other industrialized countries and have given rise to the assertion that these foreign examples validate the case for energy conservation in this country.

A recently completed effort[1] to disentangle some of the factors accounting for intercountry differences in energy-use patterns finds that things are more complex.

Although, broadly speaking, energy use has tended to show a rather strong, positive correlation with overall economic activity--judging both from the historical experience of different countries as well as from multi-country, cross-sectional circumstances at a point in time, there are numerous exceptions to that general relationship.

Specifically, America's per capita consumption of energy resources is considerably higher than it is in a number of other advanced industrial countries--e.g., France, Germany, Sweden--whose per capita income or output levels cluster within a range not appreciably different from the United States.   Consequently, the U.S. energy/output ratio exceeds by a considerable margin the ratio in numerous other countries.

---

[1]_How Industrial Societies Use Energy: A Comparative Analysis_ by me and two colleagues at Resources for the Future, Joy Dunkerley and Jack Alterman. Published for RFF by the Johns Hopkins University Press, 1977.

In interpreting intercountry energy/output variability--and particularly in considering the applicability of the findings to the United States--we need to probe the underlying reasons for such differences. Thus, we want to know whether the variability is primarily the consequence of the energy intensity that characterizes given activities within the respective economies. Or does it arise from the fact that there are important "structural" (or "mix") differences among the countries?

Note that both structural and energy-intensity characteristics of an economy may be only the surface manifestations of more deep-seated features-- e.g., geography, resource endowment, technology, demographic factors, and economic policies--which comparative analysis must address.

When economic activity and energy use in each country are broken down into principal consuming sectors--residential/commercial, transport, industry-- it turns out that by far the greatest portion of differences in energy/GDP ratios between the United States and West European countries is due to transportation. Not only are American passenger cars about fifty percent more energy-intensive (in terms of fuel per passenger mile) than European cars, but relative to given income levels, Americans also travel a lot more than Europeans.

Another contributory element is the proportionately greater share of (less energy-intensive) public transport modes in the foreign energy mix. These differences are the result not only of the much higher cost (because of taxes) of acquiring and operating cars abroad. They are also associated with urban density differentials between the United States and other countries and public policy measures resulting, overseas, in highly subsidized public transport.

Freight transport also contributes to the higher U.S. energy/GDP ratio. Interestingly, this comes about exclusively by virtue of the high volume of traffic (relative to GDP) that is generated in the United States compared to the grouping of European countries which were analyzed.

Intercountry differences in industrial energy use also contribute to the higher overall energy/GDP ratio for the United States. The industrial contribution to higher U.S. energy occurs notwithstanding the fact that our industrial sector is proportionately smaller than elsewhere. But the United States exhibits more energy-intensive production processes. What is true for the industrial sector as a whole appears to be the case also in a diverse number of specific manufacturing segments. But note that differences between the United States and other countries in industrial energy intensity need not inevitably reflect differences in the overall economic efficiency of carrying on a given industrial operation. But the findings, as far as they go, nonetheless constitute a strong presumption that U.S. industrial managers concerned with energy utilization might profitably explore the nature of foreign practices and results.

American households are, relative to income (and after adjustment for climate), bigger energy consumers than their foreign counterparts. In part, this arises from the need to provide space heating (and cooling) for larger, single-family homes. But it is also due to such practices--historically facilitated by relatively cheap fuel prices--as the heating of unoccupied rooms and the maintenance of higher temperatures. Compared to two of the countries (e.g., Canada, Sweden), U.S. insulation practices are inferior.

There is no unique factor which, in quantitative terms, can be singled out as explaining the higher U.S. energy/output ratio. Note, however, that four identifiable categories account for over 60 percent of the energy/GDP variability. In descending rank order they are: passenger transport, industry, residential space conditioning, and freight transport.

How much of this higher U.S. ratio can be ascribed with some assurance to intensity factors? Our judgment, based necessarily on incomplete data, gives a figure of around 60 percent. Even if this estimate is highly approximate it is important to recognize that intensity factors alone--that is, higher amounts of energy per unit of activity or output in the United States compared to Europe--clearly leave much of the energy/GDP variability to be accounted for by other characteristics of energy use.

In the years ahead, new conditions of energy supply and costs, new policies, and new attitudes on conservation and the environment may alter some of the historic U.S. energy-use patterns significantly, such that some of the characteristics of energy use overseas may begin to appear here. But more appropriate economic signals to energy users are probably a key ingredient in fashioning a U.S. energy picture more nearly like that else-where.

In sum, international experience as well as a reading of our own economic history suggest that the energy consumption required to provide society with a given set of amenities may display considerable flexibility. But thinking which assumes the presence of an energy-conservation ethic and abhorrence of waste "over there," in contrast to the disregard for such things in the United States, reflects notions at odds with fact and is simplistic in its view of the world.

THE SWEDISH-U.S. ENERGY USE
COMPARISON AND BEYOND: SUMMARY

Lee Schipper
Energy and Research Group, University of California
and
Energy and Environmental Division, Lawrence Berkeley Laboratory*

The study of Swedish and U.S. energy uses was conducted primarily to
compare the intensity of individual activities, taking structure and other
features into account. Several important differences in energy use efficiency were revealed, including some ripe for energy conservation. The
greatest difference between the two countries is probably in the area of
prices, but important structural, policy, and political differences exist
as well. Hopefully, the "Swedish example" will lead to U.S. investigations
of energy use technologies and conservation policies.

Several effects have to be accounted for before energy use can be
directly compared, including distance, amount of fuel extraction, climate,
and the amount of energy embodied in the goods and services making up
foreign trade. With these adjustments, the greatest differences in the
intensity of energy use appear in process heating, space heating, and
transportation.

Sweden is remarkably less energy intensive than the United States in its
space heating. This is not attributable to differences in living space/
capita (which is approximately the same as the United States) or to a
greater proportion of apartments (which are nearly as energy intensive as
single family dwellings). Fewer appliances are used in households and
buildings have greater thermal integrity.

------

*Affiliations at the time of the Workshop

In the industrial sector, the overall Swedish mix in manufacturing
is weighted more heavily toward energy-intensive products. The lower energy
intensities in Sweden are generally tied to higher energy prices, suggesting
prices affect industrial energy "needs" considerably.

The greatest contrast in energy use is in the transportation sector,
dominated in both countries by the automobile. Swedes travel 60 percent as
much as Americans and use 60 percent as much fuel per passenger mile.
Mass transit and intercity rail, which have relatively low energy intensity,
are more widely used in Sweden, while air travel, a high energy user, is
overwhelmingly larger in the United States.

Higher energy prices in Sweden than in the United States have led to
more efficient energy use. The ratio of cost of electricity to the cost of
heat from fuel was only half as great in Sweden as in the United States.
Consequently, Sweden developed a more electric-intensive technology base.
However, 30 percent of thermal electricity generation combines useful heat
with electricity. As the cost of nuclear electricity and oil go up, the
continued expansion of combined generation is certain. The effect of
different resource prices or relative efficiency of energy use is illustrated
by taxes on weight of new cars, taxes on yearly registration, and high taxes
on gasoline. The result is that total miles driven at distances less than
50 km in Sweden are less than half the U.S. figure.

While Sweden's greatest "savings" in energy consumption come from price-
related conservation, the structure of final demand also has an effect.
Institutional factors such as building codes and bank lending practices
encourage efficient structures. Savings in new structures, more efficient
industrial practices, greater use of industrial process heat, and a stabilized
ratio of 80 percent for auto/total passenger miles are to be encouraged by
government programs providing loans and grants. Assistance in cost-effective

conservation measures suggests that there is no "absolute" potential for conservation, only a level of savings to be captured, depending on prices, preferences, and institutional practices.

The real message of an energy consumption comparison between the United States and Sweden is that energy "needs" may, in the long run, be far more flexible than thought, given the differences in factors presented in this paper. The degree of flexibility may, in part, be revealed in the Swedish program for conservation.

The Swedish Conservation Campaign

Historically, Sweden has relied on her energy imports to supply nearly three-fourths of all energy used. The dramatic rise in oil prices jarred the oil-based Swedish economy, and the increasing reliance on thermal power plants assured rises in electricity prices. At the same time, the plan for increased reliance on nuclear power began to be questioned.

In response, Sweden sought a productive resolution of the energy dilemma by resolving to implement a program of energy conservation. In Spring 1975, the Swedish parliament set goals to reduce the average rate of growth to 2 percent by 1985, and to reach zero growth by 1990.

An energy conservation committee, established in Fall 1974, was assigned the task of carrying on a campaign for voluntary energy conservation, examining areas where introduction of direct restrictions may be necessary, and monitoring the development of energy use. Consumption targets for the industry, transportation, and residential/commercial sectors were established at 3 percent, 2 percent and -0.9 percent per year, respectively.

This committee is trying to influence decision makers in local govern- ments to set examples for saving energy. In industry, energy conservation folders and campaign materials are made available. Educational materials on energy conservation are now distributed to schools. A federal "Consumers Union" has examined conservation measures for households. Information on savings possibilities in agriculture has been prepared.

Administrative measures will be taken if voluntary measures fail. Investigations into different possibilities of reducing energy use in existing buildings have been undertaken. Various kinds of incentives, perhaps complemented by administrative rules, are expected to reduce space heating consumption to the 1973 level. Together with new building codes, energy consumption in buildings will probably be reduced, but not before 1985.

Industry is responsible for a good 40 percent of total energy consumption. The economic slowdown within the iron/steel and pulp/paper industries, which consumes half of all energy used in industry, brought a decrease in overall industry consumption during 1973-76, but economic recovery is needed to judge industry's needs for energy in the future.

The transport sector is growing much faster than the goal of 2 percent per year. More efficient automobiles have been suggested. The real problem of increased ownership of vehicles has not yet been dealt with.

To some observers in the United States and Sweden, the accelerated programs of conservation appear to entail sacrifices. The transition to more efficient energy use can be difficult and, consequently, the Swedish government has made nearly $1 billion available to stimulate investment in more efficient systems.

Problems in the Swedish campaign are encountered in distinguishing between lifestyle and investment as factors in conservation, as well as distinguishing between voluntary and "administrative" measures taken.

Another hazard is the stated emphasis upon yearly growth targets, rather than doing everything possible and reasonable to make energy use more efficient.   There is also a lack of unambiguous yardsticks to measure the success or failure of their goals.

Several proposals in the Carter Energy Plan resemble policies already in effect in Sweden.   It will be important for the United States to see how much and how fast government, institutional, and private initiatives can be marshalled to improve the effectiveness of energy use in Sweden.

COMPARISON OF ENERGY CONSUMPTION BETWEEN WEST GERMANY
AND THE UNITED STATES: SUMMARY

Ronald White
Stanford Research Institute

The large discrepancies between aggregate indices of energy consumption
in the United States and in certain foreign countries, and their implications
for the future welfare of various sectors of society and the economy have
been the object of considerable speculation. To understand energy use
patterns better, several disaggregated studies have been made. Disaggregation studies like these have proved controversial. Seldom have data or the
analytical methods used been questioned. Rather, it is the significance of
the findings themselves for U.S. conservation policies that has been questioned.

When U.S. per capita energy use is compared with other highly industrialized countries, and differences on the order of a factor of 2 are indicated,
this is significant and requires examination.

Closer examination reveals significant differences in the use of energy
among other countries and the United States. For example, a plentiful supply
of relatively inexpensive fuel in the United States has resulted in investment decisions that minimize capital costs at the expense of fuel efficiency.
Thus, a central issue is the disposition of present inventory before the end
of its economic life. In some cases, replacement of this inventory will
benefit present owners and therefore may be economically justifiable for them.
In many other cases the benefit will accrue to the public. It is to these
cases that considerations of public policy particularly apply.

Summary of Findings

After correction to take into account purchasing power parity rates of exchange and net exports of embedded energy items, it was found that the United States consumed about 50 percent more energy in relation to income than West Germany, rather than twice as much. We next compared West German energy use per capita with U.S. energy use per capita for the major economic sectors and subsectors. Wherever possible, we tried to distinguish among the structural factors and energy-intensive factors.

We considered the four major sectors of the economy--transportation, residential, commercial, and industrial sectors. The weighted average is 49 percent and comprises a standard of comparison for the component parts. For example, the transportation sector deviates most from the average-- 26 percent--and is thus singled out for attention in further analysis and comparison of energy use. The residential (48 percent) and commercial categories (56 percent) are closest to the average figure, and the industrial sector of Germany (61 percent) is closest to the U.S. sector is per capita use.

Next, we disaggregated the major sectors to the extent that data were available. By using reasonable equivalents of passenger-miles and freight ton-miles (which vary among the different forms of transport), we concluded that U.S. modes of transport were more energy-efficient (less energy-intensive), except for road transport. However, road transport so dominates energy use that the per capita ratios for road transport and for all transportation are nearly identical. Furthermore, it was found that the lower West German consumption could be attributed equally to fewer passenger-miles (1/2) and fewer gallons per mile (1/2).

In the residential sector, space heating dominates the list of importance subsectors. Floor space per capita in West Germany is only 64 percent
of U.S. space, and only 45 percent of that space is heated. Moreover, apartments comprise 53 percent of the dwellings in Germany versus 20 percent in
the United States. Consequently, it appears that structural factors dominate
in this subsector. The lower West German use of hot water may be accounted
for in part by the prevalence in Germany of small point-of-use heaters instead
of large central units and by a concomitant sparing use of hot water.

Factoring out per capita value of shipments accounts in some measure
for the differing scale of industrial activity, but the energy use per dollar
of shipments shipments still includes structural factors such as product mix.
The energy use per dollar of shipments for the six most energy-intensive
industries indicates lower West German energy consumption in all cases compared with the United States. Furthermore, energy use per ton of petroleum
products, steel, and paper—all relatively homogeneous products—was measured
and showed West Germany to use from 57 to 68 percent of the energy used by
the United States.

We found that "self-producers" of electricity in Germany accounted for
29 percent of the electricity generated there, whereas the comparable number
for the United States was 6 percent. This suggested, and other sources have
since confirmed, a larger incidence of cogeneration.

Structural factors are most clearly seen and understood in the residential and transportation sectors. Adding insulation to a home or rehabili-
tating a heat system are perceived as factors that improve energy efficiency,
while not affecting the basic nature of the product—a unit of shelter.
Reduction of floor space per capita and moving toward more multifamily
dwellings may be perceived to reflect a different unit of shelter. Similarly,
a more fuel-efficient automobile (probably a lighter one) may be perceived

as a different unit of transportation, although not so different as a switch
to an alternative mode such as a bus.

However, structural factors in industry present a puzzle that is much
more challenging to unravel and comprehend. Much more data and analysis will
be required to understand these structural factors well enough to analyze
the impacts of energy policy options. Despite data deficiencies that pre-
clude definitive conclusions about the relative efficiency of U.S. industrial
processes, it seems clear that U.S. industrial efficiency has been improving
since 1972.

ENERGY USE IN JAPAN AND THE UNITED STATES

Andres Doernberg
Brookhaven National Laboratory

I. Introduction

Analysis of statistics of various countries indicate that most Western European countries and Japan seem to create as many goods and services, measured as Gross Domestic Product (GDP) per capita, as the United States while consuming considerably less energy. Attempts to explain this difference and possible lessons that could be transferred to the United States have triggered a series of studies on transnational energy consumption patterns. The first one, prepared for ERDA, used Sweden as a comparison [1]. Sweden is the "ideal" subject inasmuch as its per capita GDP is the closest to the United States (and at current prices and exchange rates has surpassed it), has unique technological features such as district heat and high insulation levels, and lastly, enjoys a reputation as a model modern society. The country selected for this second study, Japan, is at the other end of the spectrum among industrialized nations. The per capita GDP is around one half of the United States (although total GDP is by far the second largest of the group of industrialized nations). Culturally, Japan is a mix between an old society different from that of the United States and a recently adopted one essentially patterned after that of the Western world. Important energy intensive sectors of industry, however, are at stages of development unparalleled anywhere else but in the United States.

Statistically, the energy consumption differences between the United States and Japan are very large. Total per capita energy consumption in

Japan is 37 percent that of the United States. Gross Domestic Product (GDP)
per capita in 1974 in Japan was 44 percent of the United States measured in
1970 prices and at the official exchange rate, and measured for the same year
with a rate (called "purchasing power parity") that is based on domestic
price levels, the GDP per capita was 63 percent of the United States. The
distinguished author and expert on Japan, Edwin O. Reischauer, asserts in his
recent book, however, that statistics such as GDP bias comparisons in favor
of Japan and do not reflect their overcrowding, cramped living quarters and
threats of environmental disaster that are inimical to an enhancement of the
"standard of living."

Per capita energy use for the residential sector is only 27 percent of
that of the United States, for transportation only 19 percent and for industry
58 percent. The differential in energy consumption for each of these sectors
is made up by elements such as Japan's larger use of passenger rail transportation, smaller consumption for space heat, more efficient iron and steel
industry, etc. These elements are all dealt with at length in the body of
this paper.

The impact of energy prices in the development of energy consumption
patterns in unclear. Until 1973 Japan actually paid less than the United States
for a barrel of crude, benefiting fully from the extensive world markets in the
sixties, while the United States had import restrictions and higher priced
domestic production. Except for historically expensive gasoline (retailing at
$1.65 per gallon in 1976) pre-1973 prices for petroleum products have been
practically identical to United States prices. No taxes are levied on heavy
oil (the principal industrial fuel) and kerosene (used for space heating).
It has to be kept in mind, however, that while Japan is fueled nearly exclusively by oil, large segments of industry and households in the United States
use natural gas which has been considerably cheaper than oil.

The prices for other fossil fuels are considerably more expensive in Japan. Coal prices on a heating unit basis have historically been more expensive than fuel oil, and the dwindling domestic production is heavily subsidized through tariffs collected on gasoline. Pipeline gas in 1974 (manufactured either from coal or LNG) was in the range of $6.50 to $7.13 per million Btu, depending on use. Considering that only two decades ago coal still constituted half of the energy supplied, the relationship between energy prices and energy thrift could be viewed as a legacy of the time when

Prices and Taxes for Petroleum Products, 1970-76

(cents per gallon)

	1970	1973	1974	1975	1976
Gasoline					
Japan					
Retail price	52	83	NA	129	165
Tax and duty	33	42	NA	35	54
United States					
Retail price	36	40	53	56	59
Tax and duty	13	12	12	12	13
Kerosene					
Japan					
Retail price	20	30	NA	48	NA
Tax and duty	2	0	0	0	0
United States					
Retail price	26	30	35	38	40
Tax and duty	0	0	0	0	0
Heavy oil					
Japan					
Retail price	6.4	11.3	NA	30.4	NA
Tax and duty	0.6	1.0	NA	0.0	0
United States					
Retail price	9.0	8.7	NA	24.7	24.4
Tax and duty	0.0	0.0	NA	0.0	0.0

Source: [1].

expensive coal was the predominant fuel source. Electricity prices are difficult to compare because of the complex pricing schemes in both countries,
but generally industrial prices have been historically comparable and
residential rates much higher than in the United States. Recent price
increases have fallen heavier on industry, weakening a policy favoring this
sector.

The industrial sector emerges as the principal focus of interest in the
study. Developing as an industrial giant since the postwar years with an
average yearly growth rate of 10 percent, Japan's plant capacity is invari-
ably more up to date than that of the United States. Complementing this
modernity is the almost total dependence on imports for both fuels and raw
materials which by itself promotes thrift.

Japan's dependence on imports of natural resources includes not only
fuels but iron ore, lead, copper, lumber, cotton, and wool. It is the
world's largest importer for all these materials except petroleum. It imports nearly all its wheat and soybeans, and 75 percent of its fish consumption originates in distant seas. Self-sufficiency in rice, a staple in the
Japanese diet, is achieved through government subsidy together with a ban on
imports. Although imports could possibly supply the market at half the price
of the domestically grown rice, they would bring about a collapse of the
agricultural sector with all the social implications this would entail.

Exports are vital for the Japanese economy and the level of international
trade is reflected in that nearly 15 percent of its consumption of direct
and indirect energy is embodied in exports. There is, nevertheless, not a
large imbalance because some 12 percent of this total energy use is embodied
in imports of nonenergy products. For the United States, international trade
represents a small fraction of total GDP and the import and export of energy
embodied in nonenergy products is balanced.

II. Energy Supply

The supply situation in Japan is drastically different from that of the United States. It is dependent on oil for nearly three quarters of its energy and essentially all of it is imported. The problem of energy supply is essentially one of oil supply, and one of the objectives of Japan's energy policy is that of diversification of sources. This remains a problem, especially since all but 5 percent of their oil comes from OPEC countries. In the first half of 1976 these were Saudi Arabia (31.4 percent), Iran (19.5 percent), Southeast Asia (17.3 percent--mainly Indonesia), and the Emirates (11.5 percent). Their non-OPEC sources are Oman and China.

Energy Supplies, 1974

	Japan		United States	
	10^{12} Btu	Percent	10^{12} Btu	Percent
Coal, indigenous	555	4	13,048	18
Coal, imports	1,957	14	--	--
Crude oil, indigenous	28	--	18,556	25
Crude oil, imports	10,290	72	7,355	10
Refined oil, imports	114	1	5,230	7
Natural gas, indigenous	106	1	23,803	33
Natural gas, imports	202	1	903	1
Hydro	824	6	2,914	4
Nuclear	204	1	1,093	2
Total	14,280		73,001	

Source: [2].

The other energy sources in Japan are coal (18 percent) used in the large iron and steel industry (half of the metallurgical coal is obtained in the United States) and which provides two thirds of the town gas used for residential cooking, hydroelectricity amounting to 22 percent of the total generated and nuclear, which in 1974 represented 5 percent of total generation

61

and by 1985 is projected to increase to 36 percent. One other indigenous
source besides solar heating is geothermal energy, which is projected to
generate 5 percent of the electricity by 1985.

III. Energy Consumption By Sectors

Energy consumption of delivered energy to the main activity sectors is
presented in the following table, and it shows for 1974 a consumption of
129 million Btu per capita in Japan versus 345 million Btu in the United
States. There are large differences in the breakdown among sectors. Japanese
industry consumes three times as much energy as the transportation sector and
two and a half times that consumed in the household and commercial sector.
In the United States these three sectors consume energy at approximately
equal levels. This difference points out the essential difference in consumption patterns between the two countries. Personal consumption of energy,

Energy Consumption by Sector, 1974

| | Japan | | United States | | Per capita |
	10^{12} Btu	Percent	10^{12} Btu	Percent	ratio (%)
Residential and commercial	2,371	17	16,786	23	27
Transportation	1.750	12	17,300	24	19
Industry	5,929	42	19,586	27	58
Other	2,661	19	14,856	20	34
Nonenergy uses	1,569	11	4,473	6	67
Total	14,280	100	73,001	100	
Population (10^6)	110.05		211.40		
Per capita energy (10^6) Btu	129		345		37

Source: [2].

which takes up the largest portion of the energy consumed in the transportation and household and commercial sectors, is much smaller in Japan, and the following sections study these in detail.

The above data are compiled as follows: the "Other" category (comprising roughly the same share in both countries) consists of stock changes, bunker fuels, transmission losses, electric generation losses and statistical differences. Industry includes all manufacturing, petroleum refining, blast furnaces gas works and natural gas processing plants. Transportation excludes bunker fuel in ships, and all military uses (which are included with commercial). Commercial also includes non-manufacturing categories not explicitly added to industry, such as agriculture, forestry and fisheries. The disaggregation differs slightly from the familiar one issued by the United States Bureau of Mines.

III-2. Industrial Sector

Japan's industrial production is the second largest of the industrialized nations, and for one of the important energy users, pig iron, its output surpasses that of the United States. The industrial sector is thus ideally suited for a meaningful comparison. It is here where technology transfer is most feasible and statements on conversion efficiency of an industrial activity in one country relative to the other are possible. Presented here are specific energy requirements for a group of energy intensive industries (iron and steel, aluminum, cement, paper). It is felt, though, that these brief intercountry comparisons by industry are merely introductory to more detailed analysis that would be required for suggestions on technology transfer.

Japan, Energy Consumption in Industry,[a] 1974

$(10^{15}$ Joule (1 Btu = 1055 Joule))

	Oil	Coal coke	Natural gas	Other gas	Purchased electricity	Total
Food	173	2	--	--	34	209
Wood and lumber	19	--	--	--	--	19
Paper and pulp	286	--	--	--	39	325
Chemicals	581	18	15	1	112	727
Stone, clay, and glass	533	21	--	1	38	593
Iron and steel	640	1,128	1	598	238	2,905
Nonferrous metals	165	35	1	1	96	298
Machinery	42	7	--	9	43	101
Transport equipment	84	1	--	14	61	160
Other[b]	243	1	--	7	124	375
Refineries	785	--	--	--	13	798
Nonenergy use	1,609	46	--	--	--	1,655
Total use in industry	5,160	1,559	17	631	798	8,165
Gas works, fuels extraction	16	21	7	27	3	74

Source: [2].

[a]Electricity at 3,413 Btu per kWhr.

[b]Mostly textiles.

64

U.S. Energy Consumption in Industry, [a] 1974

$(10^{15}$ Joule (1 Btu = 1055 Joule))

	Oil	Coal coke	Natural gas	Other gas	Purchased electricity	Total
Food	145	69	491	--	136	841
Wood and lumber	48	16	99	--	68	231
Pulp and paper	480	187	446	--	147	1,260
Chemicals and plastics	343	332	1,764	--	516	2,955
Stone, clay, and glass	132	223	713	--	104	1,172
Iron and steel	249	2,027	705	809	221	4,011
Nonferrous metals	43	38	384	--	327	792
Machinery	99	47	479	--	273	898
Transport equipment	43	45	147	--	102	337
Other	138	98	189	--	189	614
Refineries	1,897	--	1,175	--	93	3,165
Nonenergy use	3,771	221	767	--	--	4,759
Total use in industry	7,388	4,112[b]	7,359	809[b]	2,176	21,035

Sources: [3], [4].

[a]Electricity at 3,413 Btu/kWhr.

[b]Gases from coal are summed with coal and coke.

Tabulated data of energy use in industry contain all manufacturers encompassed by the US-SIC groups 20 through 39 (International SIC Nos. 31-39), which include oil refining but not gas processing, and all energy related to the iron and steel industry is included except the ancillary fuel for coking coal. Consumption of fuels for nonenergy purposes is also added.

Energy Intensity of the Industrial Mix: It is true for most economies
that the bulk of industrial energy is consumed by a small group of industries.
In the United States, the six largest (iron and steel, petroleum refining,
chemicals, pulp and paper, stone, clay and glass and nonferrous metals)
consume 75 percent of the total.   In Sweden two industries (paper and primary
metals) consume 60 percent.   In this respect, Japan is no different from Sweden.
Three industries (iron and steel, chemicals and refineries) consume over two
thirds of industrial energy, and the same six that consume 75 percent of the
total in the United States consume 86.5 percent in Japan.   Covered here are
iron and steel, aluminum (dominates nonferrous metals), pulp and paper and
cement (dominates stone, clay and glass).   Chemicals are omitted because this
category consists of thousands of products ranging from rubber to fertilizers
in which none clearly presents itself as an interesting choice for comparison.
Refineries are also omitted because a comparison of average energy consumption
per barrel would be inadequate in this category.   The mix of petroleum products
is quite dissimilar, with the United States at over two thirds of the production in light products (mainly gasoline), while in Japan two thirds of the
production are heavy oil products.

The relative energy intensity of the mix of industrial goods is comparable
between the two countries.   Measured as yearly production per capita, one set
of particularly energy intensive products, steel and cement, is greater in
Japan, while production in the United States is larger in another group that
is also very energy intensive, aluminum and paper.   The large steel production
in Japan is reflected in the large fabricated metals sector (vessels, motor
vehicles, electronic equipment), even though a sizable fraction of it is
exported.   The textiles industry, albeit not energy intensive, is larger in
Japan than in the United States.   The chemical industry linked to agriculture
(ammonia, fertilizer) is larger in the United States, while plastics production is comparable.

Production of Industrial Goods, 1973

(Metric tons per 1,000 population
 except where indicated)

	Japan	United States
Manmade fabrics	17	16
Wood pulp	93	210
Paper	147	253
Rubber	9.5	13.6
Tires (units per 1,000 pop.)	776	1,071
Ammonia	37	66
Nitrogenous fertilizers	20	44
Plastics and resins	59	57 (1972)
Oxygen gas (billion cu. ft. per 1,000 pop.)	3.1	1.9
Cement	719	372
Pig iron and ferroalloys	847	449
Crude steel	1,098	657
Aluminum, primary	10	20
Aluminum, secondary	5	4.5
Refined copper	9	10
T.V. sets (units per 1,000 pop.)	133	51
Merchant vessels (gross tons per 1,000 pop.)	144	4
Motor vehicles, passenger (units per 1,000 pop.)	41	46
Motor vehicles, commercial (units per 1,000 pop.)	24	14

Source: [5].

Iron and Steel Industry

The iron and steel industry is without doubt the most important achievement of modern Japan's industry. With a capacity as large as that of the
United States, it consumes 44 percent of the total energy in the indsstrial
sector. Together with all other steel-intensive industries such as transport
equipment and machinery, it comprises 45 percent of the total value of
shipments by manufacturing. In the United States, the latter figure is
39 percent. In 1974, Japan produced 99.6 million tons of pig iron and 129.1
million tons of raw steel; the United States in the same year produced
95.9 million and 145.7 million tons, respectively.

Inputs to Blast Furnaces: Depicted here are specific energy and

materials requirements to blast furnaces per ton of pig iron produced.   It

can be seen that Japan uses 0.441 tons   of coke per ton   of pig iron pro-

duced versus 0.609 ton/ton for the United States.   This lower use of coke is

a characteristic of Japan's steel industry, even though in the United States

the trend has also been steadily decreasing (in 1947 the ratio was 0.963 t/t).

The use of coke is replaced by higher injections of hydrocarbons and oxygen.

The figure below shows oil inputs of 1.960 million Btu per ton of pig iron in

Japan, and only 1.086 million Btu of oil and natural gas in the United States.

Inputs of oxygen are significantly higher for Japan.

The possibility of substitution between hydrocarbons and coke in the iron

and steel industry in Japan is shown in the table below, which indicates that

since the 1973 price rise in oil (and the experience of vulnerability in

supply), the use of coke has increased by 13 percent while use of oil

has decreased by 29 percent.   While part of the increase in use of coke can

be ascribed to diseconomies of scale (both 1974 and 1975 were recession years

and production was considerably under capacity), 441 kg/ton   is the largest

coke input since the early sixties; it thus clearly indicates higher coke usage.

Inputs to Blast Furnaces, 1974

Japan   United States

Fuel oil 1960MBtu/t   Oxygen   Nat. gas .306MBtu/t   Oxygen
                                       898 cu.ft/t   269 cu.ft/t
Coke .441 t/t   Fuel oil .780MBtu/t

1.367 t(ore)/t(pig)   Coke .609 t/t

                        Blast   1 ton   1618 t(ore)/t(pig)   Blast   1 ton
  72% Sintered   Furnace   pig iron   Furnace   pig iron
  9% Pellets   74% Agglomerates
  20% Iron Ore   26% Iron Ore
        Scrap .012 t/t

                                                                 Scrap .031 t/t

Sources: [6], [4].

Inputs to Steelmaking: The infrastructure of steel production is quite
different in the two countries and is a reflection of Japan's modernity. In
the United States in 1974 open hearth furnaces still produce 24.3 percent of
the total steel, compared to only 1.3 percent in Japan. The predominant
process in Japan in the basic oxygen furnace at 81.2 percent of production,
versus 56 percent for the United States. Electric furnaces have approximately
equal shares.

Japan Iron and Steel Industry, Coke and Oil
Input per Ton of Raw Steel

Year	Coke Kg/ton	Heavy Oil lt/ton
1972	390	124
1973	393	113
1974	413	102
1975	441	88

Source: [7].

Total Input, Iron and Steel Industry: A summary of total energy consumption per ton of raw steel indicates that electricity is used more inten-
sively in Japan, 1.95 million Btu (e) per ton. This is due to the configuration of the steel-making process used and the manufacture of large quantities
of oxygen gas. Expressing electricity input in terms of primary equivalent
(by multiplying by 3.0) yields a total consumption of 21.29 million Btu per
ton for Japan and 25.32 million Btu per ton for the United States. The difference is almost entirely in the use of coal. There is, however, an additional
energy savings in the case of Japan that lies hidden due to accounting convention. An indeterminate fraction of the by-product gases (coke oven and blast
furnace gases) are used as fuel by the kodo karyoku power plants which appear
as purchased electricity. This explains also the relatively small use of
these gases by the industry when compared to the United States figures. That
portion of this electricity should be accounted under self-generated power.

We can conclude then that Japanese steel is manufacutred with less than

84 percent of the primary energy requirements of steel manufactured in the

United States.

Energy Input, Iron and Steel Industry

(million Btu per ton of crude steel)

	Japan (1974 Data)	United States (1973 Data)
Coal	12.38	16.24
Oil	3.63	1.63
Natural gas	–	4.30
Purchased electricity	1.76	1.05
From utilities	1.28	
From kodo karyoku plants	.48	
Total energy (3.0xBtu (elec.)	21.29	25.32
Self-generated electricity	.19	.26
Coke oven gas	1.69	3.70
Blast furnace gas	N/A	4.42

Sources: [7], [8].

Aluminum Industry

Specific energy use in million Btu per ton of aluminum shows that elec-

tricity input to the electrolytic reduction of alumina and consumption of

carbon for electrodes is at essentially equal levels. The United States

figure of 159 million Btu primary equivalent corresponds to 7.76 kwhr/lb.,

and the Japanese data yields 7.34 kwhr/lb. Fuels strictly for process heat

are mostly natural gas in the United States and heavy oil in Japan, but other-

wise the processes used in the two countries are similar.

Alumina refining appears 24 percent less energy intensive in Japan

(19 percent of the energy is electricity while in the United States it is

13 percent). The conversion of aluminum to finished product appears twice

as energy intensive in the United States, even though the share of electricity

for this process is 68 percent in Japan and only 38 percent for the United States.

The Japanese data however makes no reference to aluminum casting, which might indicate that the difference may be due to data inconsistencies.

Energy Use Per Ton of Aluminum

(million Btu primary equivalent)

	Japan	United States
Alumina refining	25.6	35.0
Electrolytic reduction	142.7	159.0
Casting, rolling, drawing, etc.	15.0	33.4
Coal products for electrodes	26.5	28.3
	209.8	255.7

Sources: [7], [8].

Cement Industry

It is well known that the cement industry in the United States requires on the average considerably more energy than in other countries, due to the age of the existing capacity. The difference in energy use per ton of clinker between the old wet process (56 percent of United States capacity) and the newer dry process with suspension preheater (12 percent of capacity) is nearly a factor of two. The capital stock turns over very slowly because the cement business has had overcapacity for many years and the available investment funds go to pollution control equipment. In contrast, in Japan only 17 percent of capacity is by the wet process, and the suspension preheater dry method has 54 percent of total capacity and had 73 percent of total production in 1975. It is not surprising then to find that the Japanese average is 4.64 million Btu per ton versus 7.45 million Btu for the United States or 62 percent of the energy.

Energy Requirement Per Ton of Cement

(million Btu per ton)	Japan (1975)	United States (1972)
Oil	3.74	1.04
Gas	--	2.66
Coal	.09	2.40
Purchased electricity	.81	1.35
Total	4.64	7.35
Self-generated electricity	.32	N/A
Steam	.12	N/A

Sources: [7], [8].

Pulp and Paper

The pulp and paper industry is a relatively more important industry in the United States than in Japan and therefore is higher in the list of major energy users. Per capita production of pulp is 2.2 times larger in the United States and that of paper 1.7 times larger. The fact that energy consumption per ton of paper (purchased energy only) turns out to be very similar in both countries is probably linked to the relative importance of papermaking in one country versus the other. Japan as a general rule is more efficient than the United States in the industries that are important within its mix, but in less basic industries the specific energy is no better than United States use.

Most statistics within the pulp and paper industries are very similar among the two countries. In the United States, 75 percent of the pulp is made by the chemical process and 25 percent by the mechanical process; in Japan, these ratios are 72 percent and 28 percent respectively. The different paper products are manufactured in roughly the same proportions: paperboard is 48 percent of the total in the United States and 43 percent in Japan, printing and writing paper are 28 percent and 27 percent respectively, packing paper 6 percent and 7 percent, and the only large difference is in newsprint, which is 6 percent of the total in the United States and 12 percent in Japan.

Energy use per ton of paper shows a total of 23.8 million Btu per ton for Japan and 25.5 million Btu for the United States. These figures only include purchased energy. Wood by-products (liquors, bark) used as fuels would add around 60 percent to the United States use per ton, and it is probably no different in Japan. Also left out of the total is self-generated electricity, which for this industry is relatively high even in the United States.

Purchased Energy Per Ton of Paper
$(10^6$ But per ton of paper)

	Japan (1975)	United States (1972)
Oil	18.2	8.0
Coal	.1	4.2
Natural gas	–	7.6
Electricity (primary equivalent)	5.5	5.4
Purchased steam	N/A	.3
	23.8	25.5

Sources: [7], [8].

Specific energy demands per ton of paper published by Japanese sources show fluctuations through the years but no clear trend downwards. The average consumption for the last ten years is slightly lower than the 1975 figure, 22.8 million Btu, and has been as low as 21.6 million Btu per ton of paper.

III-3. Transportation Sector

The transportation sector shows dramatic differences between the United States and Japan, both in the choice of mode and in the intensity of use. More passengers are carried in Japan by railroad than by automobile, especially for longer trips. Railroads carried 40 percent of the passengers but accounted for 48 percent of the passenger kilometers, while autos carried 34 percent of the passengers and accounted for only 31 percent of the passenger kms. For

the United States, auto travel accounts for 91 percent of the total passenger
kms with air travel accounting for most of the remainder. This briefly
indicates that essentially we are observing two totally different transportation systems. There are over 9 persons in Japan per automobile, while in the
United States there are not quite 2 persons per auto. The existence of a
high speed ultramodern railroad system in Japan makes the choice between
modes quite different to that of the United States traveler faced with a
deficient railroad system and superb highways.

Transportation Energy, 1974

	Japan 10^6 Btu/cap	United States 10^6 Btu/cap	Percent
Rail, fossil	.30	2.70	11
Rail, electric	.35	.09	389
Automobile	6.6	43.6	15
Bus	.5	.5	100
Truck	5.1	21.6	24
Air	.6	7.7	8
Ship, incl. bunker	2.5	3.8	66
Total fossil	15.6	79.9	20

Source: [2].

Energy use in transportation is only 20 percent of United States per
capita levels. The largest part of this difference is travel intensity or the
amount of transportation services demanded (measured as passenger miles and
ton miles of freight). Passenger travel is only 33 percent of that of the
United States, and freight haulage only 26 percent. Clearly a large contribution to this difference originates in the distribution of the population.
The level of income clearly contributes to the difference also, but it is
not possible to separate the impacts of these two major effects.

Transportation Intensities, 1974

	Japan	United States	Percent
Passenger (per capita pass mi)			
Railroad	1,830	49	3,700
Air, domestic	99	693	14
Bus	654	296	220
Automobile	1,201	10,476	11
Total	3,784	11,514	33
Freight (per capita sh ton mi)			
Railroad	327	4,069	8
Truck	818	2,342	35
Ship	1,198	2,774	43
Total	2,379	9,185	26
Vehicles miles per auto	7,709	9,265	83
Auto efficiency (mpg)	19.0	13.8	

Sources: [9], [10]

Passenger traffic shows a predominance of rail in Japan, and the automobile in the United States. In freight transportation, truck and ship can be explained by population distribution and the relatively lower economic activity in Japan (i.e., GDP per capita) while the substantially higher use of railroad freight in the United States is probably linked to the large extractive industries absent in Japan. It is important to note that overseas freight (not included here) is an important component in Japan's transportation intensity due to imports of raw materials (fuels, ores, lumber) and exports of finished goods.

The pattern of automobile ownership is different among the two countries. According to the available statistics, automobile usage is high in Japan, 7,709 miles per vehicle per year, or 83 percent of that of the United States. This similarity in average travel is due to the existence of a sizable number of second cars in the United States that have very low yearly use (35 percent of total households have 2 or more autos), tending to depress the average. Japan consists of primarily one-car families, and their American counterparts travel relatively many more miles than the statistics tend to show. Average efficiency for the fleet of Japan's automobiles is 19.0 mpg (official sources cite 598 Kcal/pass km, at a load factor of 1.48 obtained from passenger-km and vehicle-km data). The average for the United States, obtained from fuels consumption and vehicle mile data, yields 13.8 mpg for 1974.

III-4.   Residential Sector

The residential sector typifies the difference between Japanese consumption patterns and those of the United States. Energy use in households is lower than their United States counterparts and the fuel forms are different. The barrier to a meaningful comparison is the degree to which this analysis can separate efficiency of end use devices from the satisfaction (or convenience) the United States homeowner receives from having larger homes, bigger appliances, and central heating systems.

On a per capita basis, Japanese per household consumption is less than 19 percent of that of the United States, with space heating, the largest single use in the United States, being the largest contributor to this difference at about 12 percent of United States use. The two main factors besides usage patterns are climate and size of housing. Housing size is significantly smaller in Japan, 830 sq. ft. floor area per dwelling ($77.14m^2$) versus 1,300 sq. ft. here (the United States figure refers to new construction). Single family homes in Japan comprise 65 percent of the total, and over 90 percent of the multifamily units are low-rise (under 5 stories). Climate in Japan has regional variations that are as large as those of the United States, and the bulk of the population lives in areas of average temperatures of 15°C (59°F).

Fuels to Residential Sector, 1974

	Japan		United States	
	10^6 Btu/cap	Percent	10^6 Btu/cap	Percent
Electricity	1.965	21	8.959	18
Gas[a]	3.261	35	26.396	52
Oil[b]	3.459	37	15.253	30
Other[c]	.720	8	--	--
	9.405	100	50.608	100

Source: [2].

[a]For Japan this is town gas from coal (2/3) and naphta (1/3); for the United States it is natural gas.

[b]Japan: 95 percent kerosene, 5 percent LPG; United States: 86 percent heating oil, 14 percent LPG.

[c]Coal, briquettes, charcoal, firewood.

Space heat: Homes are heated in Japan with room heaters and stoves. Very few units are centrally heated, as are 85 percent of the homes in the United States. Kerosene heats 78 percent of the total, town gas 13 percent and electricity 9 percent. One unique feature in Japan's home heating is the "kotatsu," a small heating unit (usually electric) that is present in practically all homes. It is attached under a table covered with a heavy tablecloth. People sit around the table and tuck their legs under the tablecloth. This energy-thrifty setup is an unlikely candidate for technology transfer, and is a vivid example of culture determining energy consumption levels quite independently from the concept of conversion efficiency.

Residential Primary Energy Consumption

	Japan 10^6 Btu/ household	United States 10^6 Btu/ household	Fraction
Space heating	14.4	113.6	.13
Water heating	9.5	30.1	.32
Cooking	6.4	10.6	.60
Refrigeration	4.7	11.8	.40
Lighting	3.5	11.7	.30

Sources: [6], [11].

Air conditioning: There is nearly one room air conditioner per every four households in Japan.   These consume 8.8 percent of the total electricity to the residential sector.   These units are estimated to consume 719 kwhr/ year; the estimate for the United States is nearly double, or 1,378 kwhr per room A/C.   Penetration rates are much higher in the United States, where in 1974 33 percent of all households had at least one room air conditioner and 20.6 percent had central air conditioning.

Water heating: Fewer than 1 percent of water heaters are electric in Japan, gas being the most popular, and coal, briquettes and so on still being used by 14 percent of the households.   Although omitted in official statistics, over 1 million solar water heaters have been installed in Japan.   In per household terms, Japan uses less than one third of the energy used by United States homes, most likely due to smaller units.

Cooking: The most common appliance for cooking in Japan is the gas table (90 percent saturation), while ovens are present in less than one third of the households (gas 17 percent and microwave ranges 11 percent).   The predominant fuel is gas, and when accessory items such as rice cookers (50 percent electric, 50 percent gas) are added to cooking needs, the use is 60 percent of the United States level per household.

Refrigeration: Ownership of refrigerators is at 100 percent saturation in Japan, but the units are smaller than those in the United States. Japanese data indicates 453 kwhr average electric use per year for refrigerators, while in the United States a range is given from 728 kwhr to 1,829 kwhr for 12 cubic ft. units and 14 cu. ft. frostless units respectively. Even the latter are not the largest ones available and this difference in the size of the stock accounts for Japan's average use being 2.5 times smaller. In addition, one third of the United States households have separate food freezers which are not used in Japan.

Lighting: Japanese sources cite yearly consumption per household at 296,000 kcal or 313 kwhr. Average for the United States is estimated at 1,130 kwhrs per year by Dole [11], or 3.3 times greater.

Other appliances: Japan's households are very well stocked with small appliances but average yearly consumption estimates appear consistently smaller than United States figures.

III-5. Commercial Sector

Per capita energy use in this sector appears to be at approximately the same ratio as in the residential sector (20 percent of United States levels) for Japan. The commercial sector is not well covered by United States data sources, and it becomes especially difficult to match subsectors (offices, stores, etc.) between the two countries with the available data. While data for Japan is very adequately tabulated by building types that are similar energy users, the most comprehensive data base for the United States is organized by economic activity (wholesale trade, public administration, services, etc.) and not by building type.

Energy Use, Commercial Sector, Japan, 1972

	Percent of Total Area	Percent of Energy Use	Btu/Sq.Ft.
Offices (incl. government)	9.6	15.5	59,700
Retail stores	9.1	22.4	90,600
Restaurants	.5	1.3	87,000
Amusements	1.1	3.5	113,800
Hotels, lodgings	7.6	45.5	220,000
Wholesale, warehouse	36.8	1.8	1,840
Factories	26.2	2.9	4,000
Public lighting	2.8	-	1,840
Schools, hospitals	6.1	7.1	5,500
Gas, water, sewage	0.2	-	4,000
Total	$1,428,843m^2$	$142,918 \times 10^9 Kcal$	36,800

	Energy use breakdown				
	space heat	Light & power	Water heating	Cooling	Cooking
Offices (incl. government)	.30	.51	.09	.09	.01
Retail stores	.03	.59	.10	.10	.18
Restaurants	.10	.29	.35	.05	.21
Amusements	.47	.40	.03	.10	--
Hotels, lodgings	.17	.17	.52	.04	.10
Wholesale, warehouse	.17	.66	.17	-	-
Factories	.18	.73	.09	-	-
Public lighting	.17	.66	.17	-	-
Schools, hospitals	.64	.10	.10	-	.16
Gas, water, sewage	.18	.74	.07	-	-

For two categories, hospitals and schools, there are no ambiguities in sector definition and the data can be compared. This yields overall energy consumption (per capita) for Japan of only 5 percent of the U.S. figure.

This is much lower than the 20 percent figure for the commercial sector as a whole. But further analysis into the makeup of these data reveals a problem in performing a meaningful comparison. For the United States, nearly one-half of the number of beds that are the basis for the calculation of energy consumption for hospitals belong to nursing homes, institutions which are essentially nonexistent in Japan. For schools, energy use in the United States is magnified by the inclusion of campus dormitories, which are very uncommon in Japan. It can be seen that even if consistent data were available on square footage per capita for hospitals or schools, an apparent gain of one country over another is not a measure of "standard of living" because other aspects of culture (such as elders living in institutions versus staying with families) are not equal. While a case can be made for cultural similarities among countries, for instance, in northern Europe, it is very far from being the case for Japan and the United States.

REFERENCES

1. J. S. DeHaven, "Energy Prices in Japan: A Preliminary Assessment," WN-9426-ERDA (March 1976), Rand Corporation, Santa Monica, California.

2. Brookhaven National Laboratory and Kernforchungsanlage, Julich, Data Appendix of Japan for "An Initial Multi-National Study of Future Energy Systems and Impacts of Some Evolving Technologies," BNL-50641, Jul-1406, March 1977. Also, Data Appendix of the United States.

3. U.S. Department of Commerce, Bureau of the Census, "Annual Survey of Manufactures, 1974: Fuels and Electric Energy Consumed," M74-(AS)-4.2 (September 1976).

4. American Iron and Steel Institute, "Annual Statistical Report, 1974" (May 1975).

5. United Nations, Statistical Yearbook, 1974 (New York, 1975).

6. Unpublished notes prepared by participants of the International Energy Agency Systems Analysis Project, at Brookhaven Laboratory (1976).

7. Mitsubishi Laboratories, "Quantitative Analysis of the Efficiency of Energy Consumption Within the Industrial Sector," NRC-74-1a (September 1976).

8. R. Rosen, work in progress at Brookhaven National Laboratory for ERDA AA for Conservation.

9. Ministry of Transportation, Transportation Economic Abstract (Tokyo, 1976).

10. U.S. Department of Transportation, "Summary of National Transportation Statistics," Report No. DOT-TSC-OST-76-11 (June 1976).

11. S. H. Dole, "Energy Use and Conservation in the Residential Sector: A Regional Analysis," R-1641-NSF (June 1975), Rand Corporation, Santa Monica, California.

PART II

TECHNICAL AND METHODOLOGICAL PROBLEMS

IN

INTERNATIONAL COMPARISONS

THE UNITED NATIONS INTERNATIONAL
COMPARISONS PROJECT:*   SUMMARY

Elinor Sachse
World Bank

Work on development of purchasing power parities has taken place in
three phases. Phase I covered ten countries--Colombia, France,The Federal
Republic of Germany, Hungary, India, Italy, Japan, Kenya, the United Kingdom,
and the United States--for the year 1970. The results were published in
Kravis, Kenessey, Heston, and Summers, <u>A System of International Comparisons</u>
<u>of Gross Product and Purchasing Power</u> (Baltimore, Johns Hopkins University
Press, 1975).

Phase II involved a revision of the 1970 estimates and extension of the
Phase I estimates to 1973 and expansion of the country coverage to six new
countries--Belgium, Iran, Korea, Malaysia, Netherlands, and the Philippines.
The report on Phase II is expected to be published in April 1978. Work on
Phase III has already been started and this will involve adding 16 to 20
countries, mostly developing countries, to the project. The Phase III
estimates which will be centered on 1975, are now targeted for completion in
mid-1978. Further work is going to be devoted primarily to development of
possible "reduced information" or "short-cut" methods of real GDP comparisons
for other countries and for updating benchmark estimates for all the countries
included in Phase III. In addition, planning has been started on "institu-
tionalizing" the work on international comparisons putting this work on a
regular operational basis in the United Nations Statistical Office.

---

*This is a joint project of the International Comparison Unit of the
University of Pennsylvania and the United Nations' Statistical Office.
Irving B. Kravis is Director of the project.

Several characteristics of this work were outlined:

(1) In estimating purchasing power parities the project takes an expenditure rather than a product approach though for the concerns of this conference, a product approach might have been preferable.

(2) Second, the quantity comparisons are, by and large, indirectly made. Data are collected on total expenditures in the classified groups of commodities, prices are identified for the items in that particular category, and quantities are derived from the ratio of total expenditures to unit prices. The project works with 153 detailed categories of GNP which are summarized into 34 composite categories.

(3) The definitions of GNP in the project are primarily those of the revised UN System of National Accounts. In general, inputs added into production do not represent an addition to output. For example, a potato is counted as a potato whether it took a month to grow in fertile soil with ideal climate, or several months, much fertilizer and additional applications of water.

(4) The project's practice is to base its price comparisons on equivalent specifications. Ideally, identical products across countries are sought. Lacking that, equivalent quality or, in descending order, a replication in some form of the product, or equivalence in use is used. This too affects the composition of output.

(5) Prices are market prices; they are the average prices throughout the country and averages for the full reference period. In the initial phase, the reference periods were 1967 and 1970; in the recently completed Phase II work, the reference periods are 1970 and 1973. The third phase will add 1975 as a reference year.

With regard to the results of these studies for binary comparisons there are three conventional indices. One has base-country quantity weights, and a second own-country quantity weights. Each gives somewhat different results. A third—the Fisher ideal—is merely the combination of the first two. The choice of the binary measure depends essentially on the purpose at hand. The difference between these rates and the market rate of exchange— the exchange rate deviation index—gives in proxy form a measure of the inadequacy of exchange rates as a conversion factor. It is in proxy form because the purchasing power parity ratios relate to total expenditures while exchange rates relate only to that portion of total expenditures which is traded.

In recent years, for developed countries at least, the gap between purchasing power parities and exchange rates has diminished. The main reason for this is the widespread floating of exchange rates. Despite this reduction, purchasing power parities continue to be a superior technique as they apply to all goods and not only those traded internationally.

One of the problems with binary analysis is that it is not possible to relate more than pairs of countries. If groups of countries are to be ranked in some relative standing it is necessary to move to multilateral comparisons.

There are several methods of multilateral comparison. The Geary-Khamis method, chosen by the ICP, determines international prices and purchasing power parities simultaneously for each country. International prices are the quantity-weighted average of purchasing-power-parity adjusted national prices; the purchasing power parity for each currency is the ratio of total expenditure at national prices to total expenditure at international prices. Geary-Khamus purchasing power parities differ from those derived in the binary approaches; both are an improvement over the straight conversions at market exchange rates. But the Geary-Khamis ones have the virtue of being base-country invariant: the rankings will stand no matter which country is taken as base. Moreover, a large number of countries can be put in the same comparative system.

RELATIONSHIP BETWEEN NATIONAL ENERGY CONSUMPTION AND A PURCHASING POWER INDEX: SUMMARY

E. J. Cahill and W. D. Hermann
Standard Oil Company of California

Despite the similarities of industrial societies, each is composed of a unique mixture of factors, resources and prices which dictate, within a relatively narrow range, the level of energy consumption. These economies perform many of the same tasks; yet there are many differences beneath this surface of similarity which cause energy consumption patterns to vary. The level of sophistication of international comparisons of energy consumption among industrialized countries has improved considerably. The first studies to appear applied a very aggregative measure of **Gross National Product** and energy consumption, or, at most, compared a few broad sectors of the economies such as industrial, transportation, commercial and residential. The studies tended to conclude that, while there were obvious differences among industrialized economies, they were probably minor as regards achievable energy consumption per unit of output. Subsequent research and debate have brought us to more realistic and tentative interpretations. However, there remains considerable room for improvement if policy decisions are to be based on these studies.

It is the purpose of this paper to inject a note of caution in interpreting such international comparisons. In no sense is the paper designed to provide a final answer, but rather to suggest a possible line for further study which may provide more realistic comparisons from the citizen-consumer point of view. Ill-conceived or excessively restrictive conservation measures can cause severe economic disruption and personal hardship; more importantly, perhaps, they can and will defer the search for valid, long-term solutions.

Problems of International Comparisons

One of the biggest problems in making international comparisons of energy consumption/output is deciding upon the degree of disaggregation into sectors and subsectors. The varying patterns within a sector reflect consumer preferences in goods and services and also follow established, historical patterns of international trade which, of course, are dynamic and change when comparative advantages in production change.

Consumption of complementary goods also poses real problems which differ among industrial countries. For example, while providing services such as hotel rooms, restaurant facilities and recreation may be labor rather than energy intensive, the consumption of these services relies on mobility of the user which may be much more energy intensive.

The use of exchange rates in making international comparisons also creates problems. Currency values in most countries are now permitted to fluctuate on a day-to-day basis in line with the forces of supply and demand, which means that changes in relative currency values alter the value of GNP when translated into a common currency. This leads to the simplistic conclusion that the citizens of one nation could become more affluent than those of another nation almost overnight as their currencies change in relative value. In a sense, international currency exchange rates are inappropriate for comparisons as they are based on goods and services entering foreign markets and not on the entire internal economic structure of the society. One way to avoid these problems is to compare physical units such as the amount of energy required to produce a given ton of steel. Other differences then become obvious: the different processes used, the relative age of plant capacity, the cost of cooperating factors of production. Historical cost differentials among labor, land, and capital are key elements in establishing production techniques.

Varying energy prices, including taxes, during the past quarter century only partly explain the reason for some countries' conservation practices. The necessity of some countries to earn foreign exchange to pay for oil imports provided additional constraint in energy use. A combination of geography and sense of time value also enter American consumption habits.

Purchasing Power Compared to Energy Consumption

If average annual output (converted to dollars at the average exchange rate) is compared to annual per capita energy consumption, the United States appears to be the energy wastrel, particularly when compared to Sweden. But there are more sophisticated methods of comparison which tend to measure the standard of living in a more objective manner. When average earnings are related to prices of the same items in various countries, the purchasing power of those incomes can be more satisfactorily determined and compared.

The Union Bank of Switzerland in its recently published Prices and Earnings Around the Globe has made an important contribution to purchasing power comparisons. It first selected a basket of goods and services which could be compared internationally and was readily obtained in all 41 cities surveyed. The study then examined the before and after-tax earnings of a range of clearly delineated occupations, including primary school teachers, bus drivers, and so forth. These prices and earnings were then put together to calculate the purchasing power actually existing in the 41 cities surveyed. The four U.S. cities included were the highest in average hourly earnings. As wage and salary levels are very high while prices tend to be roughly mid-way in the comparisons, employed persons in the U.S. cities have the highest purchasing power of the 41 cities surveyed.

When the purchasing power data from the Union Bank are compared with energy consumption in the countries where the 41 cities are located, they bear out the contention that energy consumption contributes to a given standard of living in an almost linear fashion. With the exception of four countries, which can easily be explained on unique grounds of energy consumption, the thirty-four countries examined show a very close linear fit in the correlation of energy consumption and purchasing power. This is particularly noticeable when Sweden and the United States are compared.

There are complex and diverse reasons for international differences in energy consumption. In the final analysis energy use contributes to what industrial societies refer to as a "standard of living." Thus, variations in energy use should be taken less as a measure of efficiency and more as a foundation which supports a given level of purchasing power.

It should also be emphasized that the relationship between energy consumption and economic output or purchasing power will change under the dictates of the marketplace as the relative prices of other factors change. This is illustrated, for example, by the already discernible decline in the U.S. ratio of energy to GNP ratio since early 1973. There are obvious areas where conservation can make a contribution to the short-term energy problem, but care must be exercised in designing policies which will induce energy savings without at the same time interfering with the economic harmony of the system. It is important that national energy policy be evolved with considerable skepticism regarding the extent to which conservation can be accomplished without jeopardy to economic performance. Furthermore, pressures which rely on incentive rather than penalty are not only likely to be more productive but have less hazard of being damaging to the economic system.

THE USES OF INPUT/OUTPUT ANALYSIS FOR
INTERNATIONAL ENERGY CONSUMPTION COMPARISONS--THE
ECE STANDARDIZED TABLES AND EXPERIENCE: SUMMARY

Joseph Smolik
United Nations Economic Commission for Europe

Input/output tables have found a significant number of applications in various national studies of the role of energy in the economic structure. The unique characteristics of this tool allow calculations to be made which are generally more difficult to obtain by other means. In particular, three types of information can be easily provided which are of current interest. First, they allow for studies of the technological and final demand structure to be made at a relatively high disaggregated sectoral level. Secondly, they provide the easiest way to calculate indirect energy requirements. Thirdly they present an alternative way to view energy flows by allowing the determination of the energy content of final products rather than by looking at energy consumption by end-use.

In order for input/output techniques to be of use in making international economic comparisons, the tables for the different countries must be standardized according to a number of criteria. In the case of the ECE tables covering twenty-one ECE countries and Japan, the objective was to standardize a set of tables according to industrial sector and by national accounting concept. The process of industrial standardization involved choosing forty-seven industrial sectors based on the ISIC which reflect the kind of commodities produced. These forty-seven sectors were felt to represent the greatest degree of disaggregation possible for the twenty-one country sample, while retaining a high level of comparability. Despite occasional mis-classifications, it is believed that a high level of comparability has been achieved.

Another important standardization criterion is the standardization of accounting concepts. Two systems of national accounting are used by ECE member governments. These two are the system of national accounts (SNA) used in the western market economies and material product system (MPS) used in the centrally-planned economies. The MPS concept is a more restrictive one since the value added on "non-materials" services is not counted as a part of GDP. Moreover, because prices are fixed by the government in the latter, certain enterprises or sectors can normally have a low -- and even a negative -- operating surplus. This characteristic is the cause of a distortion of gross value of output and value added which is more important than similar distortions due to differences in the rate of profit in market economies.

The following characteristics of standardized I/0 tables complicate international comparisons.

(1) Incomplete data for the "non-material" service sectors for most of the centrally-planned economies.

(2) The relative prices between products generally differ between countries, partly due to differences in fiscal systems. Accordingly, differences in the physical structures (both production and final demand) of two countries revealed through input/output tables reflect to a certain extent the differences in price structures.

(3) Occasionally, the actual contents of a sector are either greater or lesser in coverage than the standard.

(4)   Differences in technological coefficients between countries may reflect not only differences in relative prices, but also differences in technology and in product mix.

(5)   In general, input/output tables are published infrequently and with a substantial lag.

(6)   With regard to the use of input/output tables for energy-related work, the electricity and gas sector also includes water and sanitary services for many countries. Secondly, the tables have not been adjusted for the use of energy products and feedstocks.

A number of conclusions can be drawn from the United Nations ECE publication "Increased Energy Economy and Efficiency in the ECE Region" (Geneva, UNECE, 1976) but first it should be kept in mind that the primary objective of the I/O work in that study was not international comparisons. Rather, it was to provide some basic information which could be of use for energy-conservation studies. Consequently, the emphasis was upon identifying energy-intensive industries--those industries using large quantities of energy in production, energy-intensive final goods and final demand uses requiring significant amounts of energy.

(1)   Energy itself was found to be the most energy-intensive product in most countries in the sense that its production required relatively large quantities of energy.

(2)   As can be seen from the difference between the direct and total coefficients, relatively large quantities of energy are used indirectly to produce energy.

(3)   The large coefficients in this sector were attributed to the high energy losses involved in the conversion of energy (particularly electricity), and to the extraction, transportation and distribution of energy, which are themselves highly energy-intensive activities.

(4) The large coefficients in this sector point to the importance of shifting the structure of final demand away from energy products since the reduction of use of energy in final demand also results in a significant saving of energy by not producing it.

(5) It appears that the ranking of industries by energy intensity is similar in different countries although the size of the coefficients may vary.

Besides looking at the energy content of various products, it is also of interest to determine the relative quantities of energy required to make possible the production of the goods entering final demand. A number of observations followed from the calculations made for several countries.

(1) In all countries, energy to be used directly in final demand accounted for by far the largest percentage of total energy requirements of each country. This share ranged from 20.8 percent in Portugal to 54.8 percent in the United States.

(2) There may be significant similarities in the structure of final demand in terms of energy content between Italy and France.

(3) Exports of energy, both in their direct and embodied form, were quite large in Italy and France, accounting for 20.1 and 14.8 percent of the total energy requirements.

In conclusion, the major advantage and contribution of the ECE I/O tables is their degree of standardization by industrial sector, the number of countries included and the ease of use. The standardization of prices to allow more rigorous comparisons of structure might be a future objective, although it would certainly be a difficult one to accomplish. Secondly, foreign trade as a component of final demand (exports-imports) probably requires special attention because it represents energy flows which are not normally directly accounted for in international energy consumption comparisons. Finally, just as one might be interested in the development of E/GDP over time, it would also be useful to calculate time series of the energy intensity of the production sector as well as that of the energy intensity of final demand.

ENERGY DEMAND ANALYSIS IN THE WORKSHOP
ON ALTERNATIVE ENERGY STRATEGIES: SUMMARY

Steve Carhart
Brookhaven National Laboratory*

The Workshop on Alternative Energy Strategies (WAES)[1] analysis was per-
formed by national teams from each country using a common methodology.
Separate supply and demand studies were prepared for a range of scenario case
assumptions. For all cases, global assumptions were made concerning economic
growth, oil price, and national policy response. For the period 1985-2000,
further input parameters included additions to world oil reserves and possible political ceilings on OPEC oil production. Each national team then began
from the global assumptions and estimated appropriate national parameters.
Fuel deficits were assumed to be covered by imports, and unused domestic
supply was assumed to be available for export.

The first step in the detailed demand studies was to separate the mix
of activities from the energy intensity of each activity. Separate estimates
were made for sixty-nine sectors for both the base year of 1972 and for the
year 1985 under the various scenario assumptions. From these estimates
demand totals were built up, taking into account what types of conservation
technologies are justified by the different prices and how fast such technologies might be introduced.

---

*Formerly of WAES.

[1]Under the direction of Carroll Wilson of MIT, WAES brought together
senior decision makers from government, industry, and academia for a non-
official, ad hoc study. This was concluded in the spring of 1977 with publication of Energy: Global Prospects 1985-2000. In addition to this overview
report, WAES has published three technical volumes giving the details of the
analysis; the first of these, published in late 1976, is Energy Demand Studies:
Major Consuming Countries, which is the primary reference for the material
discussed in this paper. The other two volumes, published in 1977, are
Energy Supply to the Year 2000 and Energy Supply-Demand Integrations to the
Year 2000.

On the basis of these studies, <u>transportation</u> was found to be clearly
a far more important factor in energy consumption in North America than in
Europe or Japan. This is due to a combination of greater distances, less
fuel efficient transportation technologies, and a less efficient mix of
transportation modes. <u>Industrial</u> use is of far greater relative importance
in Europe and Japan; many industries abroad appear more energy efficient
than their American counterparts. Energy use in <u>buildings</u> is affected by
climate, population density, different standards of comfort and so on.

In the future, industrial energy growth rates are expected to approximate
overall growth rates; except for the U.S., transportation growth rates will
exceed the overall; and residential rates will generally fall below the
average. In sum, there is a reduction in the amount of energy required for
increments of GNP. Further conclusions are: (1) In response to post–1973
oil price increases, the energy coefficient associated with future growth
will be less than pre–embargo figures; and (2) further increases in energy
prices and strengthening of government conservation policies may be expected
to further reduce the energy coefficient.

The range of projected 1985 coefficients varies considerably depending
on the price level and the strength of conservation policies. It is essential
to emphasize that these coefficients are not projected on an aggregate basis
but rather at a level of detail at which individual opportunities for transfer of conservation technologies can be identified.

Individual opportunities for transfers of conservation technologies can
be identified through comparison of energy/output relationships at the detailed
level. Less efficient automobile fleets are associated with higher gasoline
prices and purchase taxes on cars. In industry, the wide range of energy use
per unit of value added can be attributed to a wide range of factors--product

mix, production technology, age of plant, plant utilization rates, to mention only a few. In general, low energy/value added figures stem from a combination of up-to-date technology and a product mix which concentrates on sophisticated product. In the residential sector, space heating dominates. Energy consumption for the purpose is influenced by climate, building standards, and heating oil prices.

The most disturbing aspect of the WAES global integrations was that for a wide variety of case assumptions, a common pattern of oil shortfall emerged. If no political production ceiling is set, then anticipated demand exceeds available supply in 1996--even with significant efforts at conservation and fuel switching. However, if political production ceilings are instituted, desired demand exceeds maximum available supply--perhaps as early as 1981.

Of course, these potential "gaps" are artifacts of the WAES methodology and will not occur in reality; supply will equal demand. However, the adjustments which will be needed to equilibrate supply and demand--at growth, price, and policy levels different from the case assumptions--may be very painful. These could include much lower economic growth rates, higher energy prices, or the need for severe energy policies.

Demand Study Conclusions

Based on the results of the WAES demand studies, several conclusions can be drawn:

1. Significant scope exists for reducing the energy/GNP relationship of the United States approaching those of Europe and Japan.

2. Significant scope exists for efficiency improvements in Europe and Japan, though not as great as in the United States.

3. Even with the substantial improvement in efficiency and fuel switching, when oil demand is compared to likely supplies, we appear to be entering a period of limited oil availability.

4. The major limiting factor in equilibrating supply and demand is the
lead times associated with large-scale supply additions or implementation
of conservation technologies.

Despite appreciable implementation of conservation technologies, the
world stands on the brink of a period in which the availability of oil supplies to meet desired demand will be uncertain and subject to political
limitations which could be imposed by a small number of critical oil producers.

What is the role of conservation in this environment? Conservation
must be pursued as part of a total program for transition from oil-based,
rapid energy growth to a sustainable energy economy based on maximum efficiency and declining oil availability. The key to achieving this transition
is acceleration of the rate of turnover of the energy-consuming capital stock.

In particular, the following programs need to be considered:

1. Methods to speed up the turnover of the automobile stock.

2. Incentives to improve energy performance of buildings or direct
    government action to improve buildings where incentives are not
    applicable.

3. Increased investment tax credits for industry.

4. Completion of a program to develop backstop technologies for oil.

5. Intensive studies of a more radical low energy growth future.

Note that these are not recommendations adopted by WAES as a group, but
rather conclusions this author has reached as a result of participation in
WAES.

METHODOLOGICAL IMPLICATIONS OF INTERNATIONAL
ENERGY DEMAND ANALYSIS

James M. Griffin
Department of Economics
University of Houston

In this paper, the salient methodological implications are outlined of
my recently completed model of energy demand in eighteen OECD countries.[1] The
fourty-five equation OECD Energy Demand Model is designed to show the effects
of fuel prices on substitution between energy and nonenergy goods and on substitution between fuels. In addition, the model relates the effects of economic
activity on the mix and level of energy consumption. The object of the model
is to provide the policy analyst with the ability to vary both fuel prices
and economic growth and to measure their impact on energy consumption. Stated
in today's most popular vernacular, the model is designed to measure the
potential for energy conservation.

The most intriguing questions in energy demand analysis focus on
medium and long-run demand relationships. Most researchers agree that in
the short-run of a year or less, energy consumption is closely tied to an
existing stock of energy-consuming equipment. Besides variation in the
utilization of the capital stock, substitution possibilities are quite limited.
Time series analysis of the short-run substitution elasticities generally
confirm this observation.

Over the intermediate and long-run, it is possible to alter the stock
of energy-consuming equipment and thereby to expand considerably the range
of substitution possibilities. Empirically, the estimation of these longer
term responses has proven a difficult task. Time series analysis of individual
countries using distributed lags to capture the capital stock adjustment

---

[1]J. M. Griffin, "An International Analysis of Demand Elasticities Between
Fuel Types," mimeo (September 1977).

mechanism faces two serious impediments. First, with an adjustment period of ten to twenty years in many cases, the shape of such long distributed lags is difficult to identify. Second, relative fuel prices and energy/non-energy prices seldom vary sufficiently in an individual country's time series sample to identify these longer run substitution responses.

For these reasons, my work in the demand area has shifted to the use of pooled international data as a means of eliciting long-run energy substitution relationships. The validity of using pooled international data to measure long-run responses rests on three propositions. First, there must exist stable empirical relationships across countries which are not affected by inherent differences between countries (which are referred to as intercountry heterogeneity). Included in intercountry heterogeneity are differences in tastes, climates, mix of output, and so forth. One need not assume the absence of intercountry heterogeneity, only the lack of a systematic correlation between it and the explanatory variables. Second, in order for international cross-sectional observations to reflect long-run equilibria, relative intra-country prices must be sufficiently stable for a country to have fully adjusted to the relative prices. Third, relative intercountry price variation must be sufficient to identify the long-run demand schedule over a sufficiently wide range.

For the eighteen OECD countries selected and the time series interval, 1955 to 1972, conditions two and three are probably met. Intracountry price variation was not great, leaving each country near a long-run equilibria. On the other hand, intercountry variation in fuel prices is largely due to differential fuel taxes. Condition one, regarding intercountry heterogeneity, is of more serious concern. Rather than to dismiss its importance, our approach has been to attempt to deal with it through the sample construction

and the explicit inclusion of variables designed to take heterogenity
into account.

The method of pooling the cross section and time series data follows
closely from the work of Houthakker.[2] As a pedagogical example, consider
the following model posited for a pooled cross-sectional, time series
sample:

$$(1) \quad y_{it} = \beta_o + \beta_1 x_{1_{it}} + \beta_{2_{it}} \qquad \begin{array}{l} i = 1 \ldots n \text{ countries} \\ t = 1 \ldots T \text{ periods} \end{array}$$

where y is the dependent variable, depending on two independent variables
x_1 and x_2. Houthakker points out that the pooled sample variation can be
separated into two separate sources of variation--"between" or intercountry
variation and "within" or intracountry variation. Model I below is the
sample dependent on the between or intercountry variation which is obtained
by analyzing the country means $(\bar{y}, \bar{x}_1, \bar{x}_2)$:

$$(2) \quad \bar{y}_i = \beta_o^b + \beta_1^b \bar{x}_{1_i} + \beta_2^b x_{2_i} \qquad \begin{array}{l} \text{Model I} \\ i = 1 \ldots n \text{ countries} \end{array}$$

The within country variation is obtained by subtracting the between country
variation in (2) from the total variation in (1):

$$(3) \quad y_{it} - \bar{y}_i = \beta_o^w + \beta_1^w (x_{1_{it}} - \bar{x}_{1_{it}}) + \beta_2^w (x_{1_{it}} - \bar{x}_{2_{it}}) \qquad \begin{array}{l} \text{Model II} \\ i = 1 \ldots n \\ t = 1 \ldots T \end{array}$$

Note that Model I depends on the cross-sectional variation while Model II
reflects the time series variation the the n countries. From the above
discussion, it follows that the β_i^b of Model I reflect long-run responses,
while the β_i^w of Model II reflect short-run responses.

---

[2]H. S. Houthakker, "New Evidence on Demand Elasticities," _Econometrica_ (April 1965) pp. 277-288.

Even though our principal concern is with Model I, Model II was also estimated. The within country variation does serve as a test of the hypothesis that short-run substitution responses are quite limited. Furthermore, the within country sample serves as a weak test for bias due to intercountry heterogeneity in the between country model. Intercountry mean differences, which would include intercountry heterogeneity as well as relative price differentials, are eliminated in Model II. If the short-run substitution response in Model II approach or exceed the long-run responses obtained from Model I, the between country results in Model II are biased downward due to intercountry heterogeneity.

Since for forecasting purposes it is desirable to describe the adjustment path from the short to the long-run, still a third model was estimated. If a distributed lag were introduced into (3) to reflect lagged effects of x, then the sum of the lagged coefficients should approximate the long-run coefficients reflected in β_i in Model I. In effect, Model III utilizes a pooled dynamic sample, utilizing a distributed lag (w) in the time series component,

$$(4) \qquad y_{it} = \beta_0 + \beta_1 \sum_j w_j \, x1_{i,t-j} + \beta_2 \sum_k w_k \, x2_{i,t-k} \qquad \begin{array}{l} \text{Model III} \\ i = 1 \ldots n \\ t = 1 \ldots T \end{array}$$

Since $\sum w_j = 1$, then $\beta_i \overset{\sim}{=} \beta_i^{\,b}$. Similarly, one would expect that $\beta_1 w_0 \overset{\sim}{=} \beta_1^{\,w}$. Model III was used in the OECD Energy Demand Model because of its dynamic properties. The empirical results did in fact confirm that $\beta_i = \beta_i^{\,b}$. The short-run responses $(\beta_i^{\,w})$, however, tended to be considerably smaller than $(\beta_i \, w_0)$ suggesting that Model III tends to overstate the short-run response.

Given the selection of a pooling procedure, the next critical question was to formulate a specification by which both energy/nonenergy substitution and interfuel substitution occurs. In view of the structural differences

between energy-consuming sectors, it was deemed necessary to devise an approach
which could be applied separately to the electricity generation, industrial,
residential, and transportation sectors. For a given sector, it would be
desirable to determine interfuel and energy/nonenergy substitution simultaneously. For example in the industrial sector, the production technology
would posit that industrial output (Q) depends on capital (K), labor (L),
materials (M), and fuel inputs $(E_1 ... E_m)$ as follows:

$$(5) \quad Q = f(K, L, M, E_1 ..., E_m)$$

To estimate a production relationship which would allow for variable elasticities
of substitution among the inputs, detailed data on the prices of K, L, and M
would be needed in addition to fuel prices.

To circumvent these data requirements, it was assumed that energy input
(corrected for thermal efficiency differences) constitutes an aggregate, so
that fuel determination occurs at two stages. In equation (6), aggregate
energy demand is determined:

$$(6) \quad Q = f(K, L, M, E)$$

Subsequently, the mix of fuels is determined:

$$(7) \quad E = g(E_1, E_2, ... E_m)$$

In empirical applications, equation (6) is taken to be a CES technology to
avoid the data problems. Equation (7) utilizes as a dual to the energy
aggregate, the energy cost aggregate approximated by the translog function,
which allows for variable fuel substitution elasticities.

While data limitations necessitate the two-step approach in (6) and
(7), it should be recognized that the approach requires the assumption

that fuels are weakly separable, a sufficient condition for which is:

$$\sigma_{KE_1} = \sigma_{KE_2} \cdots = \sigma_{KE_m}$$

$$(8) \quad \sigma_{LE_1} = \sigma_{LE_2} \cdots = \sigma_{LE_m}$$

$$\sigma_{ME_1} = \sigma_{ME_2} \cdots = \sigma_{ME_m}$$

There is mounting industry-specific data showing that the substitution elasticity conditions are not met. For example, in electricity generation, nuclear fuel and capital are complements while fossil fuels and capital tend to be substitutes.[3] While at an aggregate level, the bias may not be large, it remains an unanswered question.

The issue of energy separability is a manifestation of a more general problem in international energy demand modeling: to what degree should a _priori_ theoretical conditions be imposed in work of this type. Unlike pooled data within a country for a specific industry, the analysis here utilizes broad aggregates across countries. The theoretical strictures of microeconomic theory become tenuous. In fact, it is probably more appropriate to interpret (6) and (7) as reasonably stable empirical relationships rather than as "the" production function and "the" energy aggregate as the existence of such as this stage of aggregation can be seriously questioned.

If one accepts the interpretations of these functions as stable empirical relationships, it does not follow that microeconomic theoretical conditions are irrelevant. Stable empirical relationships imply the working of certain underlying forces, in this case market forces. For example, market forces would not allow the consumption of one fuel to be determined irregardless of

---

[3]J. M. Griffin, "Long-run Production Modeling with Pseudo Data: Electric Power Generation," _Bell Journal_ (Spring 1977) pp. 112-127.

the consumption of other fuels; therefore, some theoretical framework such as in (5), (6), and (7) is necessary.

The critical question is not the absence or presence of economic theory, but the degree to which theoretical conditions are imposed. The more theoretically restrictive the formulation, the greater the sacrifice in explanatory power over the sample period. While sample period fit is not the only criteria for model validation, it is important. Moreover, the gain from the added theoretical restrictions is uncertain, depending on its superiority in future forecasting and policy simulation exercises. Thus there would appear to be a trade-off between theoretical restrictions and forecast performance.

To illustrate the dilemma, one specification did not proceed from an explicit energy cost aggregate, but merely hypothesized that fuel cost shares obey linear homogeneity in fuel prices and the accounting identity that cost shares sum to unity. A second specification based on (7) utilizes fuel cost shares which impose these conditions. In addition, the parameters must also obey the condition that the product of the cost shares (S_i) and the cross price elasticities (E_{ij}) are equal (for example, $S_i E_{ij} = S_j E_{ji}$). The first specification yields a considerably better sample fit. On the other hand, the elasticity condition in the second specification is important as it prevents good B from being a complement to good A, if good A is a substitute for good B.

Questions of this nature pose a significant and often overlooked problem to the model builder. Too often the economist disregards less restrictive specifications because of their lack of a rigorous theoretical basis. Frequently, noneconomists tend to commit the opposite and more serious mistake of constructing models and analyzing energy relationships without the insights offered by economic theory. Too often these differences are obfuscated by all parties agreeing that the central problem is data availability.

PART III

THE KEY SECTORS--BUILDING,
TRANSPORT, INDUSTRY

INTERNATIONAL COMPARISONS OF INDUSTRIAL
ENERGY UTILIZATION: SUMMARY

Robert S. Spencer
Industrial Consultant

Making international comparisons of energy usage simple enough to be
meaningful is a difficult task. The methods used in analysis should be
formulated around the purpose of the analysis. Recently, this purpose has
been the formulation of national energy policy. But comparisons made at
the aggregate level are of minimal use to industry in improving its energy
utilization efficiencies. Rather, comparisons need to be made almost at the
manufacturing plant level and sometimes between specific operations in a
manufacturing process.

Suggestions About Methodology

"Product mix" is an idea which is often used qualitatively and loosely,
rather than clearly defined. A "product mix" is the division of the totality
of some activity into a set of categories which are significant in the given
context. In our case, the activity is the output of an economy or sector
of an economy, and the categories are the various goods and services which
are provided. This is not quite as simple as it sounds, as the definition
of the categories can be very dependent on just what kind of decisions are
to be made. But having defined the categories, we can describe the output
quantity vector, whose dimensionality is equal to the number of goods and
services we have defined, as making up the output of our economy.

Many business managers think of the quantity vector as a combination of
two concepts, physical volume and product mix, and want to separate quantitatively changes in these two components. In general, this is not possible,

except where the totality is quite homogeneous. The difficulty is in specifying a single scalar quantity as "volume," because of the wide variety and non-additivity of units.

Managers will want to quantify mix changes by reducing them to a scalar quantity, and will want to know if changes in mix are desirable or undesirable. In order to quantify mix changes and permit value judgments, another factor must be brought in, some measure of merit or value, such as energy intensities. The simplest case takes value added during each defined operation as the measure of quantity. The ratio of energy consumed to the output of the economy can then be written

$$r = \sum_i e_i f_i \text{ , or } = \vec{e} \cdot \vec{f}$$

where f_i is the fraction of the entire GNP or Gross Domestic Product contributed by the i-th good or service, and e_i is the energy consumed per dollar of the contributed GNP or GDP.

Since comparisons of various countries with the United States are to be made, the subscript "0" for the U.S. and "1" for the other country can be used. In this situation it also seems appropriate to use the Laspeyre type of formula for an index of comparative energy intensity, thus,

$$E = (\vec{e}_1 \cdot \vec{f}_0)/(\vec{e}_0 \cdot \vec{f}_0)$$

Now since the index comparing the overall ratios is

$$R = (\vec{e}_1 \cdot \vec{f}_1)/(\vec{e}_0 \cdot \vec{f}_0)$$

and if we define a mix index, M, such that

$$R = (E)(M)$$

then the mix index is given by

$$M = (\vec{e}_1 \cdot \vec{f}_1)/(\vec{e}_1 \cdot \vec{f}_0)$$

We then take the ratio of the two scalars to give us our index of comparison. This approach of decomposing the energy/output ratio into multiplicative factors instead of additive factors avoids the problem of the so-called interaction term (which is hard to explain when questions arise).

The foregoing kind of analysis is not very useful to an industrialist who is concerned about the energy efficiency of his manufacturing operations. This requires an expansion of our formulas. But applying these formulas to actual inter-country comparisons is another matter, for physical quantities are needed. This means that comparisons cannot be made by using a small number of categories at a high level of aggregation, but only using categories that are relatively homogeneous.

Studies which have made comparisons of conditions in the year 1972 have pointed out that most of the Western European countries were experiencing average energy prices about double that in the United States, which would tend to lower the ratio of energy to output. Since the cost of energy is a relatively small fraction of total GDP, the effect would be negligible for the total economy, and would not even amount to much for the entire industrial sector. For energy intensive industries, such as primary aluminum, however, the effect becomes significant and should be taken into account in any analysis.

Industrial Sector Comparisons

The management of energy is not the only concern of most industrial managers. The manager strives to arrive at a balance according to his objectives of all factors going into his operations. What the average manager has seen in the past as an optimum balance has seldom in the United States been heavily weighted toward minimum energy use.

Conservation can be achieved through good "housekeeping" practices like insulation and improving maintenance. Beyond these, there is a whole spectrum of energy saving opportunities which cover a range of investment from replacement of process equipment to rearranging parts of the manufacturing process.

In the United States there has been a steady improvement in industrial energy used, when adjusted for level of production since 1971. But the impact of varying levels of utilization of production capacity on industrial energy consumption should be noted. A close connection between process efficiency and the rate of growth in production might be expected but here again lack of homogeneity in industry category can make measurement difficult.

Conclusions

(1) Some industrial operations are probably less energy efficient than corresponding operations in other industrialized nations, but these differences are probably less than they were five years ago and will continue to narrow.

(2) Improvement in the industrial sector is less a matter of learning from other nations' experience than a matter of adequate economic motivation. Even with considerable motivation, improvements in energy efficiency in industry take time.

(3) International comparisons of industrial energy usage should be done by examining energy consumed per physical unit of production. This means conducting the analysis at a relatively low level of aggregation. When necessary to conduct the analysis at a relatively high level of aggregation, the outputs must be expressed in common units.

(4) International comparisons of industrial energy efficiencies should take into account all the other factors which can be expected to have an impact on operating efficiencies.

(5) The primary purpose of such comparisons is to provide background and guidance to the formulation of national energy policy. This should be kept in mind in study design.

AN INTERNATIONAL COMPARISON OF ENERGY AND MATERIALS
USE IN THE IRON AND STEEL INDUSTRY*

Gideon Fishelson and Thomas Veach Long, II
Committee on Public Policy Studies
The University of Chicago

Introduction

In one of the first publications to suggest the value of international
comparisons in exploring possible substitutes for energy and materials use,
Berry, Long, and Makino [1] discussed the production of polymers, aluminum,
steel, and paper in the Netherlands, the United Kingdom, and the United States.
Similar technological investigations have formed the focus for a continuing
program at the University of Chicago [2]. In the past two years, a portion
of this effort had been in cooperation with the NATO Committee on Challenges
of a Modern Society, Industrial International Data Base Project, in which
one of us (TVL,II) participates as chairman of the Methodology Group. In
section I, we report in a telegraphic fashion some of the technological
results of the CCMS pilot study of the steel industry [3] as amended by research
at Chicago.

Since the inception of this research, we have been aware of the desir-
ability of coupling the precise technological description derived from an
engineering approach to a framework for economic evaluation. Below we present
our initial attempt at this merger. Section II contains a discussion of a

*The authors gratefully acknowledge the support of this research by the
U.S. Department of Energy, Division of Industrial Energy Conservation.

This report was prepared as an account of work sponsored by the United
States government. Neither the United States nor the United States Department
of Energy, nor any of their employees, nor any of their contractors, sub-
contractors, or their employees, makes any warranty, express or implied, or
assumes any legal liability or responsibility for the accuracy, completeness
or usefulness of any information, apparatus, product or process disclosed,
or represents that its use would not infringe privately owned rights.

time-series, cross-national econometric analysis of factor substitutability in the iron and steel industry. The treatment, which utilizes a translog cost function specification of the industry's technology, allows us to explore the extent to which factor price differentials have influenced production decisions involving energy and materials use. As will be seen, there appears to be large substitutional possibilities for both energy goods and raw materials.

Section I

Pig iron and crude steel production data for eight principal western steel-making nations are given in table 1. The most significant observation is the large portion of world production furnished by the United States and by Japan, a relatively new entrant in the international iron and steel market. The two principal processes in steel-making are the production of pig iron in a blast furnace and the subsequent production of steel in a steel furnace. The product of the blast furnace is hot blast furnace metal, and the energy consumed in producing one metric ton of hot metal in these countries is found in table 2. As we can observe, the United States uses considerably more energy than other nations in hot metal production, but the extent to which this is of concern to energy policy-makers depends upon an evaluation of the supply of coal suitable for use in coke production.

Juxtaposition of the first and second columns in table 2 calls our attention to the need to establish definite conventions in carrying out an analysis of energy use and to compare results under different sets of conventions. In the first column of that table, the energy values do not include the energy required to produce coke that is purchased by the iron and steel industry. In other words, the combustion enthalpy for purchased coke is not adjustable for the coking efficiency. However, the energy that is used in the production

of coke from coal on-site is included. In the second column, the total energy
consumption figure reflects an evaluation of all the coal energy that is
required to produce both the purchased and self-produced coke in the steel-
making process based on the national average coking efficiency reported by
the self-producers. In the third column, one finds the energy required for
ore preparation prior to its injection into the blast furnace. This would
include the energy for pelletization, the primary preparation step in the
United States, and for sintering, the predominant method in other countries.

In table 3, the energy consumed in producing a metric ton of crude
steel is displayed. The energy value given includes the energies required
for the blast furnace step and those required for the various steel furnaces
employed. These are national averages. In comparing tables 2 and 3, one
notes that the energy required for the blast furnace step in Italy is greater
than that in the Federal Republic of Germany. Yet, the total energy required
for the production of steel in Italy is less than that used in the FRG. The
key to this apparent anomaly can be found in column 4 of table 3, under the
heading "Hot metal ratio." This percentage gives the ratio of hot metal to
total iron (including scrap steel) injected into the steel furnace. As one
can see, approximately 55 percent of the Italian production is produced using
scrap steel, with only 45 percent produced from hot blast furnace metal. In
the conventions adopted in the studies of Ref. [3], scrap is assigned a zero
energy value, and the Italian production techniques appear more energy
efficient than the German techniques due to the higher scrap input. However,
one must be concerned over the long-term availability of scrap in an
international market. Data on scrap purchases and use in steel production
are contained in table 4.

The observed differences in energy required for steel production are
only partially attributable to differences in scrap utilization. Another

major determinant of energy and materials use is the steel-making technology

employed. In table 5, the percentage of crude steel produced using the three

principal steel-making technologies--open hearth, basic oxygen, and electric

furnace--in each of the countries is shown. Data is also included for the

relatively small amount of steel produced using a Thomas furnace. In table 6,

the energy used in each of the steel-making furnaces is shown. Again, the

accounting convention in which scrap is assigned a zero energy value is

employed. Thus, the electric furnace, which accepts a 100 percent scrap

injection, appears to be much more energy efficient than either the open

hearth or the basic oxygen furnaces. Relatively large scrap charges can

also be used in an open-hearth facility, but the maximum injection for the

basic oxygen process is approximately 25 percent. As one can observe, in

the two newest technologies--the basic oxygen furnace and the electric

furnace--the United States is reasonably energy efficient. However, for the

older open hearth furnaces, which still account for approximately 25 percent

of United States production, the high energy use is noteworthy.

Section II

This study is one of a series aimed at evaluating the potential for

factor substitution in energy-intensive industries. The principal inputs of

interest are energy and raw materials. Due to the complexity of the produc-

tion process, these two inputs cannot be studied in isolation, and their inter-

actions with capital and labor must be considered.

The cross-national investigations focus on two levels of aggregation.

Initially, we examine the aggregate manufacturing sector, and then we turn

to specific industries. The industries are iron and steel, chemicals,

pulp and paper, and petroleum refining. Although we experiment with a Cobb-

Douglas function, the emphasis is on use of translog cost and production functions [4,5,6,7,8,9]. This analytical choice has the notable advantage that few a priori constraints are thereby imposed, except that of the functional form. Hence, the data, which reflect the aggregate behavior of the economic agents, are as free as possible to tell the economic story. We note the Cobb-Douglas and the CES functions are special cases of the translog function.

Below we present a comparison of factor use in the iron and steel industry, based on pooled cross-national, time-series data. In addition to the availability of reasonably accurate data, there are other factors that motivate our choice of this industry as a "test case." First, in the United States, only the petroleum and coal products industry uses more energy per employee, per dollar of value added, and per dollar of output than the primary metals sector, of which the iron and steel industry is a major part. Second, output is relatively homogeneous across countries, and production processes are few and well defined (blast furnace, and open hearth, electric, and basic oxygen process steel-making). Finally, casual observation indicates that steel prices appear to be strongly correlated with energy prices.

The data presented in Appendix A indicate considerable variation in the energy/employment ratio and in the energy/output ratio for this industry across countries. How can these differences be explained and justified economically? This is the task of this study. Our findings point to a single explanatory variable--the difference in input price ratios.

Assumptions and Methods

Attempts to analyze the differentials in energy/GDP ratios between countries by disaggregating energy usage and GDP into various sectors of the economy indicate which sectors are responsible for the overall difference, but they do not explain the sources and the reasons for the sector difference [10]. Interestingly, Alterman and others argue that the dispersion of the energy/value-added ratio over nations is "narrower for the industrial

sector than for other energy-using sectors." [10] Their intuitive explanation

is that, "after all, we are dealing for the most part here with a group of

highly advanced economies which suggests roughly comparable if not identical

degrees of industrial penetration and with countries none of which is denied

the energy-using manufacturing processes and other technologies that flourish

elsewhere." [10] However, even if technologies are identical, two firms

(countries) will employ identical factor proportions only if the price ratios

of the inputs are identical. Conversely, even if the technologies differ,

price ratios exist that would lead to identical factor ratios. These state-

ments are based on the assumption of rational profit-maximizing behavior by

producers.

The basic assumption underlying the study is that the production of iron

and steel in different countries can be characterized by a single common pro-

duction function. A priori this assumption is difficult to justify, and it

can be confirmed or disproved only on empirical grounds. Similarly, there

is no prior justification for the specification of a translog functional

form. The reason it is used is its relative generality and easiness of

application.

Denoting output by Q and the quantity of input i by X_i, $i = 1 \ldots n$; then

the translog function takes the form:

(1) $\ln Q = \ln \alpha_0 + \sum_{i=1}^{n} \alpha_i \ln X_i + \frac{1}{2} \sum_i \sum_j \gamma_{ij} \ln X_i \ln X_j$

in which α_0, α_i, and γ_{ij} are the parameters of the function. The technical

derivations of the relations to be estimated are given in Appendix B. The

equations to be estimated are the factor shares of the inputs. They are

related either to "modified" value added (value added plus the cost of energy)

production and cost functions or to the total output production and cost functions. The main reason for employing several estimation procedures is to check for consistency. The elasticities of substitution for the pairs formed by capital, labor, and energy should have the same sign and be of the same order of magnitude in each of the four estimation procedures.

Data

Assembling and analyzing international data is considerably more difficult than evaluating intracountry figures. In addition to total absence of data, questions related to data homogeneity arise. Once these are solved, a major task is bringing the variables that are measured in money units, usually at domestic current prices, to a comparable base. For variables that are measured in physical units (manhours, tons of coal, barrels of oil, and so forth), this difficulty does not arise; however, there might be quality differentials that should be taken into account (for example, male-female labor force participation, level of education, age enthalpies of combustion for generically similar fuels, capital vintages, and so forth). Griffin and Gregory [9] argue for low inter-country and intertemporal variance in labor quality indices and in capital depreciation rates.

The models tested include the variables: capital, production labor, other labor, energy, and materials. Data bases must be developed for each of these variables.

The proper exchange rate for converting money values into a common unit is the specific by-variable-by-country-by-year purchasing power parity. Need-less to say, complete information of this type does not exist. The most detailed purchasing power data for a year within the analyzed time series, 1963-1973, are found in the Kravis and coauthors study [11]. However, they do not cover all the countries included in our sample, nor the specific output and input variables that we employ, and their study is limited to 1970. The procedure we adopt is as follows. The year 1973 is chosen as a "benchmark" year, and we assume that the exchange rates for that year are in the same ratio as the purchasing power parities. The advantage of choosing 1973 is that the majority of countries included in the analysis had already entered the currency float, but the large price increases resulting from the oil embargo had not yet passed through the system. A synthetic exchange rate is then calculated by adjusting the official rate by the ratio of the price index in a given country to that in the United States. For example, for the year 1970, the synthetic exchange rate Ex_i for country i results from:

$$(1970 \ Ex_i') = (1973 \ Ex_i) \left(\frac{1973 \ U.S. \ Price \ Index}{1973 \ Country \ (i) \ Price \ Index}\right)\left(\frac{1970 \ Country \ (i) \ Price \ Index}{1970 \ U.S. \ Price \ Index}\right)$$

in which Ex_i' is the synthetic rate, while Ex_i is the official rate. Comparing the synthetic exchange rates for 1970 resulting from this procedure with the more accurate purchasing power parity values of Kravis and coauthors [11] indicates that the differences are tolerable--not greater than 20 percent. Note that by choosing one year as a benchmark and continuously adjusting the official exchange rate as above, the ratio between the synthetic exchange rate and the true purchasing power parity rate is a constant for each country over time, but differs among countries.

The most severe problem is the lack of capital data. While the share of capital in total cost can be inferred from the difference between value added and labor payroll (including supplements), we do not have data for quantities and prices for capital. Thus we adopt the following procedure. Figures for gross fixed capital formation in current prices and in 1970 prices adjusted by the 1970 official exchange rates are available. The ratio between the two capital formation series is divided by the 1970 official exchange rate. The result is a price index (1970 = 100). By multiplying this price index by the interest rate that is releveant for manufacturing investment ($r_{it}/100$),

the capital cost is annualized [12]. The product of the two is taken to
be the net capital price index. From United States data for the manufacturing
sector, we calculate an implicit cost of capital that is approximately eight
times the relevant interest rate (the ratio of gross returns to capital/gross
book value of structures and equipment). Thus, denoting the net capital price
index of country i in year t by C_{it}, the gross capital price index is assumed
to be eight times C_{it}, denoted by I_{it}. The quantity of capital employed is
implied from the returns to capital and its price; that is:

$$(2) \quad \left(\frac{[\text{Value Added}]_{it} - \text{Labor [Payroll + Supplements]}_{it}}{[\text{Index of Capital Price}]_{it}} \right)$$

The value of the numerator must be measured in United States constant (1970)
dollars in order for the capital stock to be in United States 1970 dollars.
The transformation to the United States constant dollars is done by dividing
the variables in the numerator that are measured in domestic current prices
by the product of the 1970 synthetic exchange rate and the domestic price
index where 1970 = 100.

The price of labor is calculated as the ratio between labor payroll and
labor quantity. One difficulty lies in the division between production and
other workers of the supplements to wages that are part of labor costs. Futher-
more, supplements-to-wages data are not available for all years. This
adjustment is significant because of the relatively large share of the supplements in the total returns to labor. In the absence of additional information,
the supplements were distributed in proportion to the number of workers in
each group. The calculated cost per unit of labor is then converted to
United States constant prices by dividing it by the product of the 1970
synthetic exchange rate and the GDP price deflator (1970 = 100). Labor and
labor costs are taken from United Nations data [13].

Energy consumption figures for the manufacturing sectors in tons of oil equivalent are available in an OECD publication [14], and we utilize this without further correction for efficiency in use. They are classified into solid fuels, petroleum products, natural gas, and electricity. The prices associated with each are from an unpublished FEA data base. The prices are in current domestic currency for a domestic unit of measurement. We associate the price of coal with solid fuels, and of heavy oil with petroleum products. For natural gas and electricity, specific price data for each are available. The prices are those paid by industry. The prices, after conversion to a per-ton-of-oil equivalent, are further transformed to United States constant prices by the same procedure used for labor prices. The total energy price is a weighted average (by quantity) of the various fuels and electricity prices $(\sum_j P_j Q_j / \sum_j Q_j)$.

Explicit data on quantities of raw materials are available only for steel scrap. One method would define expenditures on raw materials to equal the difference between value of output and value added. This definition then includes the expenditures on energy goods in those for raw materials, and in order to find the expenditures on nonenergy raw materials, the energy cost has to be subtracted. The construction of a price series for raw materials is by using the following ratio:

$$P_{rm} = \frac{\text{Output (Current Domestic Prices)}}{\text{Output (Fixed Domestic Prices)}}$$

$$\frac{[(\text{Value Added} + \text{Energy Costs (Current Domestic Prices)})]}{[(\text{Value Added} + \text{Energy Costs (Fixed Domestic Prices)})]}$$

The real quantity of raw material is the value of the denominator of the price equation divided by the exchange rate. An alternative that is pursued is to investigate a modified value added function, excluding raw materials as Griffin and Gregory did [9].

The last variable is output. The more homogeneous the analyzed industry is, the better is its output measure. For the iron and steel industry, even quantity data of physical outputs are available. Yet the factor share equations require output data in value units. These are readily available as value added (at factor cost), but not always for total output. Output can be calculated as an aggregate product of the quantitative output of the type of steel and its price.

The factor shares by definition are independent of the conversion to constant United States prices and thus are calculated using domestic current prices. The shares are taken either with respect to modified value added, measured at factor costs, or with respect to output costs, measured at factor costs. Since the latter information is not always available, the difference between output at factor cost and at market prices is captured by the raw materials input. In countries where the two diverge, the measure of raw materials is biased, and it embodies the difference between taxes and subsidies to industrial production. However, given the data problems discussed above, estimating the elasticities of substitution from the cost function share equation is the less demanding in terms of data.

Estimation Procedure

The estimation should be done jointly for the complete system of factor share equations, since they are related by common constraints ($\Sigma\alpha_i = 1$, $\gamma_{ij} = \gamma_{ij}$, $\sum_i \gamma_{ij} = \sum_i \gamma_{ij} = \sum_{ij} \gamma_{ij} = 0$), and the error terms are not independent. However, due to the definition of factor shares ($\Sigma M_i = 1$), the sum of the error terms is identically zero. This makes the variance-covariance matrix singular and prohibits the estimation of the entire system. In Appendix B we show the solution, which results from the elimination of one of the equations. The symmetry constraints must yet be fulfilled, and the error terms are likely to be correlated. Thus, the Zellner three-stage estimation is called for. The problem, however, is that the resulting estimators are not independent of the equation that was eliminated. The alternatives are to use either maximum likelihood estimation or an iterative Zellner three-stage procedure. The latter is asymptotic maximum likelihood, which explains its use by other researchers [6,9,15]. We prefer to use the maximum likelihood estimation procedure. The algorithm is that of Wymer.[1]

The elimination of one equation changes the explanatory variables of the factor share equations derived from the production function to input ratios and those derived from the cost function to price ratios. Hence, the calculated variables for the cost function estimation are independent of the conversion of the prices to base year prices and to a common unit of accounting. They are the ratios of the observed or calculated domestic current prices. Thus, using the cost equation factor shares saves some strong assumptions and presumably makes the estimation more accurate.

Results

Caveat: All results that are given in tables 7-9 are being reevaluated. Do not use these values quantitatively. They are included only to indicate the type of results that will be generated.

The order in which the results are presented is the following. First, we provide the conventional Cobb-Douglas production functions for modified value added and for total output; then the maximum likelihood estimations of the translog cost functions are presented. Table 7 contains the Cobb-Douglas results. The important features are:

---

[1]The algorithm was kindly furnished to the University of Chicago by Mr. Wymer of the London School of Economics.

(1) The sum of the elasticities is significantly above unity; for example,
the iron and steel industry does exhibit increasing returns to scale
for the value added function.

(2) The elasticity of energy is significantly above its factor share,
while that of capital is significantly below its factor share. The
estimated elasticity for labor fluctuates. It seems that the proper
specification for a modified value added function distinguishes
between production workers and other labor.

(3) A time variable that represents Hicks neutral technological progress
appears to be significant, indicating a progress rate of value added
of about three percent per year.

(4) The explanation is high, reaching 98 percent.

For the total output function, the governing input becomes raw materials.
It loses its overwhelming effect only when country dummy variables are included,
but their inclusion produces an artifically low capital elasticity, while
labor is somewhat too high. The interesting result for this case is that the
sum of the elasticities is not significantly different from unity, while
the explanation reaches 99.8 percent.

In general, the results of the Cobb-Douglas specification indicate that
there is little to gain from relaxing constraints, that is, from allowing
the elasticities of substitution to take values other than unity. For the
translog specification, we present the maximum likelihood estimates for the
total output cost function in table 8. The results are presented in a matrix
form. It is interesting to note the small order of magnitude of the coefficients,
which are very similar to those presented by Griffin and Gregory [9]. On the
other hand, coefficients seem to be much more significant, based upon the ratio
between the coefficients and the corresponding standard errors. The implicit

elasticities of substitution estimated for the United States for 1971 are
presented in table 9.

Although a comparison with other studies is not straightforward due to
differences in the industry and the input definition, some results can be
used as indicators. The labor-capital elasticity of substitution is somewhat
below unity and is between that estimated by Griffin and Gregory (0.06) [9]
and those of Berndt and Wood (1.01) [4], Hudson and Jorgenson (1.09) [5],
and Humphrey and Moroney (0.73) [15]. We find that capital is a likely
substitute for all inputs except energy. The same is true for nonproduction
labor. Raw materials are substitutes for labor, but they are strong complements
to energy. On the other hand, labor and energy are complements. The latter
results contradict Griffin and Gregory's findings [9]. The unreasonable
result is the own elasticity of substitution of energy--a positive sign. Yet
it is very similar to the one found by Hudson and Jorgenson [5].

TABLE 1

Pig Iron and Crude Steel Production Data

(All Data in Million Metric Tons)

	Pig iron		Crude steel	
	1970	1973	1970	1973
Belgium	11.0	12.8	18.1*	21.4*
France	19.1	20.3	23.8	25.3
Federal Republic of Germany	33.6	36.8	45.0	49.5
Italy	8.4	10.1	17.3	21.0
Japan	76.1	92.7	93.3	119.3
Netherlands	3.6	4.7	5.0	5.6
United Kingdom	17.7	16.8	27.9	26.7
United States	85.1	91.5	119.3	136.8
TOTAL:	254.6	288.2	349.7	405.6
Percent of World Production	59.3	58.1	58.9	58.2

*Includes production data for Luxembourg. In 1973, approximately 72 percent of the combined production shown above was made in Belgium and the balance in Luxembourg.

Sources: "The Iron and Steel Industry in 1973 and Trends in 1974," Organization for Economic Cooperation and Development, Paris (1975).

Annual Statistical Report, 1974, American Iron and Steel Institute, Washington, D.C. (1975).

TABLE 2

Energy Consumption for One Ton   of Hot Blast Furnace Metal

Units: Gigajoules (GJ) Per Ton   of Hot Metal

Country	Total energy consumption	Total energy consumption with all coke evaluated at national self production efficiency	Energy required for oil preparation
Belgium	27.779	27.8	2.843
France	25.689	35.4	4.449
Federal Republic of Germany	21.460	24.2	2.393
Italy	24.509	24.6	2.209
The Netherlands	23.688	24.7	2.157
United Kingdom	27.544	27.8	2.237
United States	30.464	30.8	4.269

Source: Ref. [3]as modified and amended at the University of Chicago.

TABLE 3

Energy Consumption for One Ton of Crude Steel

Country	Total energy input GJ/t	Credit for gas after steel-making GJ/t	Net energy (2) consumption GJ/t	Hot metal ratio %
Belgium	23.767	n.d.	n.d.	81.5
France	20.812	2.400	18.412	74.6
Federal Republic of Germany	16.735	2.252	14.483	71.5
Italy	14.889	2.086	12.803	45.4
The Netherlands	20.139	3.449	16.690	80.7
United Kingdom	19.589	n.d.	n.d.	53.3
United States	21.828	1.312	20.516	61.7

Source: Ref. [3].

TABLE 4

Scrap Indexes and Ratios for One Ton of Crude Steel

Country	Total scrap kg/t	Recycled scrap kg/t	Purchased scrap kg/t	Imported over purchased scrap %	Exported scrap kg/t
Belgium	305	231	74	25.7	n.d.
France	344	208	136	n.d.	n.d.
Federal Republic of Germany	395	200	195	14.0	44.5
Italy	632	230	402	66.7	0.5
The Netherlands	287	212	75	n.d.	n.d.
United Kingdom	500	200	300	n.d.	18.0
United States	469	256	213	0.6	59.7

Source: Ref. [3].

TABLE 5

Percentage of Crude Steel Made with Different Processes

Country	Processes			
	Thomas furnace and others	Open hearth furnace	Basic oxygen furnace	Electric furnace
Belgium	14.61	1.47	79.90	4.02
France	24.50	13.04	51.76	10.70
Federal Republic of Germany	2.94	17.65	69.61	9.80
Italy	———	14.80	43.80	41.40
The Netherlands	———	1.61	92.22	6.17
United Kingdom	0.80	27.50	43.20	23.50
United States	———	24.36	55.96	19.67

Source: Ref. [3].

TABLE 6

Energy Consumption for One Ton of Liquid Steel Produced with Different Processes

COUNTRY	THOMAS FURNACE & OTHERS Energy consumption GJ/t liquid steel (scrap/hot metal charge)	OPEN HEARTH FURNACE Energy consumption GJ/t liquid steel (scrap/hot metal charge)	BASIC OXYGEN FURNACE Energy consumption GJ/t liquid steel (scrap/hot metal charge)	ELECTRIC FURNACE Energy consumption GJ/t liquid steel
Belgium	26.893 (14/86)	5.400 (100/0)	23.492 (24/76)	not comparable
France	27.252 (4/96)	12.759 (74/26)	22.422 (23/77)	5.170
Federal Republic of Germany	22.207 (9/91)	12.443 (69/31)	19.014 (21/79)	4.377
Italy	——	19.025 (45/55)	21.956 (21/79)	6.775
The Netherlands	——	5.893 (100/0)	20.466 (20/80)	5.523
United Kingdom*	28.675 (48/52)	20.810 (47/53)	24.188 (24/76)	5.285
United States	——	23.929 (41/59)	24.776 (26/74)	6.537

(*) Figures refer to 1 ton of ingot steel.

Source: Ref. [3].

TABLE 7

A. Cobb-Douglas Production Functions Elasticities of Production[a]

Dependent Variable—Modified Value Added

I.	Total Employment	.369	(.046)
	Capital	.279	(.066)
	Energy	.585	(.039)
	$R^2 = .945$		
II.	Total Employment	.385	(.045)
	Capital	.324	(.067)
	Energy	.568	(.039)
	Time	.037	(.015)
	$R^2 = .948$		
III.	Production Workers	.512	(.185)
	Other Labor	.185	(.190)
	Capital	.222	(.052)
	Energy	.335	(.041)
	$R^2 = .978$		
IV.	Production Workers	.578	(.184)
	Other Labor	.109	(.189)
	Capital	.250	(.053)
	Energy	.349	(.041)
	Time	.024	(.011)
	$R^2 = .980$		

B. Dependent Variable—Total Output

I.	Total Employment	.101	(.033)
	Capital	.152	(.029)
	Raw Materials	.642	(.040)
	Energy	.232	(.023)
	$R^2 = .990$		
II.	Total Employment	.112	(.034)
	Capital	.162	(.030)
	Raw Materials	.633	(.040)
	Energy	.231	(.023)
	Time	.009	(.007)
	$R^2 = .990$		

C. Same Dependent Variables, but with Country Dummy Variables

Total Employment	.346	(.047)
Capital	.054	(.021)
Raw Materials	.287	(.034)
Energy	.346	(.036)
$R^2 = .998$		

a) The output elasticity for an input is the percent change in output per one percent change in the corresponding inputs. $E_i = \frac{\partial Q}{\partial X_i} \cdot \frac{X_i}{Q}$. Values in parenthesis are standard errors of estimates.

Table 8

Iron and Steel Industry

Factor Shares Output Maximum Likelihood

Estimation of Total Output Cost Function

The Eliminated Equation is Capital Share.[a]

	Constant	PRICE Prod. Work.	PRICE Other Labor	PRICE Raw Mat.	PRICE Energy	PRICE Capital
Production Workers	.239 (.022)	.052 (.006)	-.014 (.003)	-.002 (.010)	-.029 (.005)	-.007
Other Labor	.046 (.013)	-.014 (.003)	.021 (.002)	-.005 (.005)	-.001 (.003)	-.001
Raw Materials	.887 (.053)	-.002 (.010)	-.005 (.005)	.097 (.022)	-.125 (.010)	.035
Energy	-.409 (.029)	-.029 (.005)	-.001 (.003)	-.125 (.010)	.161 (.007)	-.006
Capital[b]	.237	-.007	-.001	.035	-.006	-.021

a). Values in parenthesis are asymptotic standard errors.

b). Implied from the constraints:

$$\Sigma \alpha_i = 1$$

$$\sum_j \gamma_{ij} = \sum_i \gamma_{ij} = \sum_{ij} \gamma_{ij} = 0$$

TABLE 9

<u>Elasticities of Substitution, the Iron and Steel Industry</u>

<u>United States — 1971</u>[a]

	Production workers	Other labor	Raw materials	Energy	Capital
Production workers	-2.07	-00.54	.99	-1.64	.83
Other labor		-11.80	.72	.33	.82
Raw materials			-.56	-4.40	1.43
Energy				7.80	.12
Capital					-4.49

a) $\sigma_{ii} = \dfrac{\gamma_{ii} + M_i^2 - M_i}{M_i^2}$

$\sigma_{ij} = \gamma_{ij}/M_i M_j + 1$

APPENDIX A

International Comparison of Input-Output Ratios

Iron and Steel — 1970

Country	Energy[a] (MTOE)	Employment[b] (10^3)	Value Added[b] ($\$10^6$)	Output[b] ($\$10^6$)	Energy Employment	Energy Output
Austria	2.09	62.6	377.7	987.4	.033	.0021
Belgium	6.08	125.0	853.3	———	.049	———
Canada	4.51	65.0	992.3	2160.9	.069	.0021
Denmark	10.14	5.7	45.1	103.6	.025	.0013
Greece	0.46	3.8	42.0	139.0	.121	.0033
Federal Republic of Germany	22.55	678.0	7280.0	13737.3	.033	.0016
Ireland	0.04	12.2	55.4	131.9	.003	.0003
Italy	7.03	188.0	1741.2	4499.7	.037	.0016
Japan	42.34	549.0	5612.2	18648.7	.077	.0023
The Netherlands	2.47	80.0	436.3	2085.2	.031	.0022
Norway	2.02	15.1	136.8	301.0	.135	.0067
Spain[c]	3.30	84.0	729.1	2271.0	.039	.0015
Sweden	2.37	56.6	678.8	1457.8	.042	.0016
United Kingdom	16.33	472.0	2887.3	7230.2	.035	.0023
United States	54.07	891.0	14580.0	31980.1	.061	.0017

a) OECD, Energy Balances 1960-74, Paris, 1976.

b) U.N., Growth of World Industry, 1973, New York, 1976.

c) 1971 data.

APPENDIX B

Technical Description.   The Translog Function

The technical specification of the translog production function describes the relation between physical output and inputs:

$$(3) \quad \ln Q = \sum_{1=1}^{n} \alpha_i \ln X_i + \tfrac{1}{2} \sum_{ij}^{nn} \gamma_{ij} \ln X_i \ln X_j,$$

in which Q denotes output, X_i the quantity of input i, and α_0, α_i, and γ_{ij} are the parameters of the function.   The equality $\gamma_{ij} = \gamma_{ji}$ is necessary for the applicability of the integrability condition.   The translog specification, like the Cobb-Douglas, requires that $X_i > 0$ i = 1...n.   Without imposing additional constraints and by adding an error term to equation (3), the parameters can be estimated by applying ordinary least squares procedures, since the model is linear in the parameters.   In addition to the question of whether the input quantities are truly exogeneous, the disadvantage of direct estimation is the large number of parameters (for a three-input model there are ten) and possible high correlations among the inputs.   Furthermore, as with other production function specifications, direct estimation does not utilize all the information that is conventionally available, such as factor prices.

To assume constant returns to scale in the controllable inputs implies that:

$$(4) \quad \Sigma \alpha_i = 1$$

$$\Sigma \gamma_{ij} = \sum_{j} \gamma_{ji} = \sum_{j} \gamma_{ji} = \sum_{ij} \gamma_{ij} = 0$$

Although these constraints can be easily imposed in the direct estimation procedure, reducing the number of parameters, and lessening the severity of the multicolinearity, we would still not have utilized all the maximum information. In order to incorporate all the available information, an indirect estimation procedure is adopted.

The marginal product of input i is:

$$(5) \quad F_i = \frac{Q}{X_i} \left(\alpha_i + \sum_j \gamma_{ij} \ln X_j \right)$$

Hence:

$$(6) \quad F_{ii} = \frac{Q}{(X_i)^2} \left(\gamma_{ii} + [\alpha_i + \sum_j \gamma_{ij} \ln X_j - 1] \, [\alpha_i + \sum \gamma_{ij} \ln X_j] \right)$$

One would expect $F_i \geq 0$, $F_{ii} \leq 0$. The second-order cross partial derivatives are:

$$(7) \quad F_{ij} = \frac{Q}{X_i X_j} \left(\gamma_{ij} + [\alpha_j + \sum_k \gamma_{ik} \ln X_k] \, [\alpha_i + \sum_k \gamma_{jk} \ln X_k] \right)$$

The assumption of positive marginal product can also be expressed in the form of positive elasticities of production. Given the logarithmic specification of the production function, the elasticity of production is:

$$(8) \quad \frac{\partial Q}{\partial X_i} \cdot \frac{X_i}{Q} = \alpha_i + \sum_j \gamma_{ij} \ln X_j \geq 0$$

In contrast to the Cobb-Douglas function where the elasticities are constant, independent of the quantities of inputs, in the translog function they have a constant part and a variable part. The latter depends upon the quantity of all inputs.

In competitive factors and product markets, the value of the marginal product of an input equals input price (P_i). When output is measured by value of output (that is, physical output multiplied by a unique price when output is of one kind, or, a sum of products of quantities and prices when more than one output is produced) in equilibrium, total production costs equal the total value of product. Hence,

(9) $F_i = P_i$ and $C = \Sigma Q_j \cdot P_j$.

Denoting factor share in total cost by M_i and the elasticity of production by E_i, one finds that:

(10) $M_i = \dfrac{P_i X_i}{C} = \alpha_i + \underset{j}{\Sigma} \gamma_{ij} \ln X_j = E_i$

The assumption of constant returns to scale assures that $\overset{n}{\underset{i}{\Sigma}} M_i = \Sigma E_i = 1$. The marginal rate of substitution between two inputs is defined by:

(11) $R_{ij} = F_j / F_i$

Recall that at equilibrium, $F_j / F_i = P_j / P_i$. Allen [16] defined the partial elasticity of substitution between inputs i and j by:

(12) $\sigma_{ij} = (\underset{i}{\Sigma} F_i X_i / X_i X_j) \; (|\bar{F}_{ij}| / |\bar{F}|)$

where $\bar{F}$ is the matrix of second-order conditions and $\bar{F}_{ij}$ is the ij cofactor of that matrix. Because the first- and second-order derivatives of a translog function are not independent of input levels, the elasticity of substitution is also not independent of input levels. This is the major difference between the translog and the CES function.

For practical purposes, insufficient data forces us to assume various degrees of separability. Weak separability between inputs i, j, and k requires that the ratio F_i / F_j be independent of the level of k. Hence, a change in the quantity of input k changes the marginal productivities of inputs i and j in the same proportion. This also implies an identical elasticity of sub-stutition between k and i, and k and j. From the definition of the marginal rate of substitution, we find that the condition for separability is accordingly:

(13) $F_i F_{jk} - F_j F_{ik} = 0$

Introducing into this expression the values of the first and cross derivatives (from above) and the definition of factor shares, we find that the separability condition is identical to:

(14) $M_j \gamma_{ik} - M_i \gamma_{jk} = 0$

While the γ_{ij} are parameters of the production function (that is, constants independent of input prices), the factor shares depend on input intensities which depend on input prices. Thus, any conclusion about separability applies only locally. An a priori assumption that all input combinations are separable over the whole range of observations is a global restriction that does not necessarily hold, and should be tested. On the other hand, the assumption of separability is sometimes necessary when data are incomplete. For example, we have information on value added and energy employed in production, but not for value of raw materials. Correspondingly, let us denote the labor input by L, capital input by K, energy input by E, and other raw materials by N. Then:

(15) $Q = f(L,K,E,N)$

Consider the variable denoted by V, which is specified by

(16) $V = g(L,K,E)$

We have to assume that:

(17) $Q = f(V,N) = f(g[L,K,E],N)$

implying separability between L, K, E, and N when data on N are not available. In this study we are concerned with the parameters of (15) but settle for the parameters of (17), when necessary.

Given the identify between factor share and production elasticity, we
find for the translog specification of (15) that:

(18) $M_L = \alpha_L + \gamma_{LL}\ln L + \gamma_{LK}\ln K + \gamma_{LE}\ln E + \gamma_{LN}\ln N$

$M_K = \alpha_K + \gamma_{KL}\ln L + \gamma_{KK}\ln K + \gamma_{KE}\ln E + \gamma_{KN}\ln N$

$M_E = \alpha E + \gamma_{EL}\ln L + \gamma_{EK}\ln K + \gamma_{EE}\ln E + \gamma_{EN}\ln N$

$M_N = \alpha N + \gamma_{NL}\ln L + \gamma_{NK}\ln K + \gamma_{NE}\ln E + \gamma_{NN}\ln N$

When relation (17) is assumed, the fourth equation and the last column to the
right ($\gamma_{iN}\ln N$) are eliminated from (18) and the M_j are defined correspondingly.
(Note that in all instances $\sum_j M_j = 1$.)

Relations (15) and (17) are not deterministic; neither are the equations
of (18). However, due to the constraint $\sum M_j = 1$, the sum of the random effects
for each observation equals zero by definition, which makes the system singular.
Also note that the disturbance term of (15) is not identical to those in (18).
The identify holds only when the disturbance of (15) is heteroskedastic; that
is, it is of the following nature:

(19) $U = \sum_i^n w_i \ln X_i,$

where U is the disturbance term of (15) and w_i are the disturbances of (18)
(i = L,K,E,N).

In addition to the singularity problem we encounter a set of restrictions
on the production function: constant returns to scale ($\sum \alpha_i = 1$) and symmetry
of the cross parameters ($\gamma_{ij} = \gamma_{ji}$). Imposing these restrictions on equation
(18) enables the reduction of (18) to a system which is lower by one degree
and is nonsingular. For example, one possible solution reflecting the
constraint is:

(20) $M_L = \alpha_L + \gamma_{LL} \ln(L/N) + \gamma_{LK} \ln(K/N) + \gamma_{LE} \ln(E/N) + U_L$

$M_K = \alpha_K + \gamma_{KL} \ln(L/N) + \gamma_{KK} \ln(K/N) + \gamma_{KE} \ln(E/N) + U_K$

$M_E = \alpha_E + \gamma_{EL} \ln(L/N) + \gamma_{EK} \ln(K/N) + \gamma_{EE} \ln(E/N) + U_E$

System (20) contains all the relevant information available about the production process (output and input prices and quantities). For each additional input (labor can be divided into skilled and unskilled, capital can be divided into structures and equipment, energy can be divided into oil, gas, coal, electricity, and so forth), an equation and a right-hand column are added.

Until now we have discussed the characteristics and implied estimation properties of the production function. Alternatively we could have investigated the characteristics and the implied estimation properties of the cost function associated with the production function using the powerful Shephard lemma [17]. What is needed is the cost function associated with the specific translog production function. Admittedly we do not know it, but we assume that regardless of the functional form of the production function the cost function is translog (the production function is not a translog).

Correspondingly, instead of investigating the elasticities of production and the elasticities of substitution between inputs in production, we investigate the cost elasticities and the elasticities of substitution between inputs in the cost function. The links between the two estimations are the assumptions of competitive product and input markets and the rational economic behavior of cost minimization for any level of output by the producers. The analysis of the cost function thus reveals the technical parameters of the production function.

A translog cost function is a logarithmic Taylor expansion of the general cost function:

(21) $C = C(Q, P_i)$ $i = 1 \ldots n$

such that:

$$(22) \quad \ln C = \beta_0 + \beta_1 \ln Q + \beta_2 (\ln Q)^2 + \sum_i^n \delta_i \ln P_i + \tfrac{1}{2} \sum \sum_{ij}^{nn} \delta_{ij} \ln P_i \ln P_j + \sum_i^n \psi_i \ln P_i \ln Q$$

For the translog function to preserve the general characteristics of a well behaved cost function (that is, linear homogeneity in factor prices), the following relations should hold:

$$(23) \quad \sum_i \delta_i = 1$$

$$\sum_i \delta_{ij} = \sum_j \delta_{ij} = \sum_{ij} \delta_{ij} = 0$$

$$\sum \psi_i = 0$$

The last condition plus those that $\beta_i = 1$, $\psi_i = 0$, $i = 1 \ldots n$, and $\beta_2 = 0$ fulfill the requirement of a production function with constant returns to scale.

Employing the second part of Shephard's lemma [18]:

$$(24) \quad X_i^* (Q, P_i) = \partial C / \partial P_i$$

where X_i^* is the optimal value of X_i; that is, it is the level along the path of minimal cost [16]. As in the production function analysis, we find that:

$$(25) \quad E_i = \frac{\partial \ln C}{\partial \ln P_i} = \frac{P_i}{C} \cdot \partial_C / \partial P_i$$

From (22), (23), and the constant returns to scale assumption

$$(26) \quad \frac{\partial \ln C}{\partial \ln P_i} = \delta_i + \sum_j \delta_{ij} \ln P_j$$

Hence:

$$(27) \quad \frac{P_i}{C} \cdot X_i^* = M_i^* = \delta_i + \sum_j \delta_{ij} \ln P_i$$

M_i^* is the cost share along the minimum cost path. The actual cost share is M_i, where:

(28) $M_i = M_i^* + e_i$

e_i is a random disturbance. Thus, the observed factor equation is a stocastic relation. Returning to the four inputs production function discussed above, the corresponding factor share equations based upon the cost function (22) are:

(29) $M_L = \delta_L + \delta_{LL}\ln P_L + \delta_{LK}\ln P_K + \delta_{LE}\ln P_E + \delta_{LN}\ln P_N + e_L$

$M_K = \delta_K + \delta_{KL}\ln P_L + \delta_{KK}\ln P_K + \delta_{KE}\ln P_E + \delta_{KN}\ln P_N + e_K$

$M_E = \delta_E + \delta_{EL}\ln P_L + \delta_{EK}\ln P_K + \delta_{EE}\ln P_E + \delta_{EN}\ln P_N + e_E$

$M_N = \delta_N + \delta_{NL}\ln P_L + \delta_{NK}\ln P_K + \delta_{NE}\ln P_E + \delta_{NN}\ln P_N + e_N$

The restrictions imposed on the factor share equations (29) are identical to those imposed upon (20). The singularity problem remains. By reducing the system to the following three equations system, the constraints are fulfilled and the singularity problem resolved:

(30) $M_L = \delta_L + \delta_{LL}\ln(P_L/P_N) + \delta_{LK}\ln(P_K/P_N) + \delta_{LE}\ln(P_E/P_N) + e_L$

$M_K = \delta_K + \delta_{KL}\ln(P_L/P_N) + \delta_{KK}\ln(P_K/P_N) + \delta_{KE}\ln(P_E/P_N) + e_K$

$M_E = \delta_E + \delta_{EL}\ln(P_L/P_N) + \delta_{EK}\ln(P_K/P_N) + \delta_{EE}\ln(P_E/P_N) + e_E$

Note that the fourth equation is eliminated.

The elasticities of substitution implied from the cost function are [15]:

(31) $\sigma_{ij} = C(\partial^2 C/\partial P_i \partial P_j)/(\partial C/\partial P_i)(\partial C/\partial P_j) = \dfrac{C \cdot C_{ij}}{C_i \cdot C_j}$

Using the formula for the first- and second-cross derivatives of the cost function, when expressed in terms of factor shares renders:

(32) $\sigma_{ij} = \delta_{ij}/M_i M_j + 1 \qquad i \neq j$

(33) $\sigma_{ii} = (\delta_{ii} + M_i[M_i-1])/M_i^2$

Furthermore, defining the cross price elasticity by μ_{ij}, where:

(34) $\mu_{ij} = \dfrac{\partial \ln X_i}{\partial \ln P_j}$

and by applying Allen's findings [16], we express the input demand elasticities in terms of factor shares and elasticities of substitution:

(35) $\mu_{ij} = M_j \sigma_{ij}$

and:

(36) $\mu_{ii} = M_i \sigma_{ii}$

Hence, using the estimators of system (29), we are able to calculate the elasticities of a substitution and the corresponding elasticities of demand for inputs.

REFERENCES

1. R. Stephen Berry, T. V. Long, II, and H. Makino, Energy Policy vol. 3,
    (1975) p. 144.

2. See T. V. Long, II, "International Comparisons of Industrial Energy Use,"
    to be published in the Proceedings of the NSF-Mitre Workshop on Long-Run
    Energy Demand (1976).

3. NATO/CCMS Report No. 47; Pilot Study, The Steel Industry, U.S. Department
    of Energy (1977).

4. E. R. Berndt and D. O. Wood, Review of Economic Statistics vol. 57, p. 254
    (1975).

5. E. A. Hudson and D. W. Jorgenson, Bell Journal of Economics vol. 5, p. 461
    (1974).

6. M. A. Fuss, Journal of Econometrics vol. 5, p. 89 (1977).

7. M. Denny amd D. May, Journal of Econometrics vol. 5, p. 55 (1977).

8. F. G. Adams and J. M. Griffin, "Energy and Fuel Substitution Elasticities
    Results From an International Cross Section Study," UN Economic Research
    Unit, UN Conference on Trade Development (August 1974).

9. J. M. Griffin and P. R. Gregory, American Economic Review vol. 66, p. 845
    (1976).

10. J. Alterman, J. Darmstadter, and J. Dunkerley, How Industrial Societies
    Use Energy: A Comparative Analysis
    (Baltimore, Johns Hopkins University Press for Resources for the Future,
    1977).

11. I. B. Kravis, Z. Kenessey, A. Heston, and R. Summers, A System of Inter-
    national Comparisons of Gross Product and Purchasing Power (Baltimore,
    Johns Hopkins University Press, 1975).

12. The data are from OECD, National Accounts Statistics, 1974 (Paris, 1976)
    and OECD, Interest Rates, 1960-1974, Financial Statistics (Paris, 1976).

13. United Nations, <u>Growth of World Industry</u>, 1973 (New York, 1976).

14. OECD, <u>Energy Balances</u> (Paris, 1976).

15. D. B. Humphrey and J. R. Moroney, <u>Journal of Political Economy</u> vol. 83, p. 57 (1975).

16. R. G. D. Allen, <u>Mathematical Analysis for Economists</u> (London, Macmillan, 1938).

17. R. W. Shephard, <u>Cost and Production Functions</u> (Princeton, Princeton University Press, 1953).

18. R. W. Shephard, <u>Theory of Cost and Production Functions</u> (Princeton, Princeton University Press, 1970).

CONSERVATION AND TRANSPORTATION –
THE PRIMARY ISSUES: SUMMARY

R. Eugene Goodson
Purdue University

The discussion in this paper pertains primarily to the United States. Recent studies projecting energy demand and transportation through the early part of the twenty first century have varied widely in their totality.   The primary differences turn out to be in automobile travel, air travel, and energy shipments. Related parameters are the fuel economy of the automotive fleet, the growth rate in light-duty trucks and vans, personal income growth rates, and the potential for continued decentralization of our population.

Various international projections have indicated that the primary worldwide energy conservation measure probably lies with the United States automotive fleet. I conclude that the main worldwide, most volatile energy demand factor in transportation is in the air sector. In the United States, air transportation growth was very high in the mid-1960s, often exceeding 16 percent per year. Rising incomes make such a continued growth in air travel highly likely.

Automobile travel in the United States has for many years not changed appreciably in the number of miles per person per year. Major growth in the per capita automotive transportation is unlikely.

There seems no such constraint in the air transport mode. In one scenario in the Committee on Nuclear and Alternative Energy Systems (CONAES) study, air transport growth projects to air travel miles per capita reaching almost 50 percent of auto travel miles per capita by the year 2000.

Historically, transportation in the United States has consumed approximately 14 percent of personal expenditures. Of this, the vast majority goes to automobiles. But, as incomes rise, as auto travel saturates, and as air transportation costs reduce with increasing efficiency (which is likely), air transportation energy demand and travel could grow substantially in the United States and dramatically across the rest of the world. In underdeveloped countries, it is a different matter entirely. The demand for autos seems to rise dramatically as incomes increase. Energy transport around the world may be a potential high-growth factor in transportation.

Uncertainty in Making Projections

Since the main issues in transportation energy demand are automotive travel in the United States, air travel in the developed countries, and auto ownership in the developing countries, what data are available to analyze those growth potentials? The world data base to analyze air travel potential and automotive ownership probably does exist. We might be in much better shape in predicting automotive energy demand in the United States, but there are several unknowns, such as controversy over the elasticity of demand for gasoline as a function of its price.

It seems clear that the short-term elasticity of gasoline demand is almost entirely a function of travel demand elasticity. It also seems clear that long-term energy elasticity is dependent upon new car fuel economies that preceded the fuel-use estimate period by several years.

The potential for new car fuel economy improvements is large. It seems clear that there will be a doubling in average fuel economy in the United States over the next twenty years, at little sacrifice in interior volumes, comfort and convenience, and with little or no cost increase for new automobiles anticipated in real terms.

153

As automobile efficiency doubles, travel energy costs at energy prices
will halve. Therefore, gasoline prices would have to double in real terms
to keep auto travel energy cost constant. There is very little data for
automobile energy demand at half current travel cost.

One might ask if automobile fuel economies will actually double in the
next twenty years. The technology is in hand, unless the most stringent
emission standards are enacted. The 1975 Energy Policy and Conservation
Act requires 27.5 miles-per-gallon new car average fuel economy by 1985. A
major issue, however, is whether such fuel economy will occur, even with the
Act, if gasoline prices remain constant.

Conclusions

The primary issues seem to be:

- What level of automotive energy conservation can be
  achieved in the United States?

- What level of air travel growth will occur worldwide,
  particularly in those areas where automobile travel is
  saturating?

- What level of automobile ownership growth will occur
  in developing countries?

- What are radically new technologies or transportation substitutes
  (such as telecommunications) which may have major effects on
  transportation energy demand?

Issues which are reaching resolution are:

- The potential for mass transportation energy conservation is not
  large and to occur would require major changes in living
  patterns, urban densities, and public subsidy of mass transportation.

- The potential for rail transportation to capture a significant portion
  of trucking at increased energy efficiency is low.

RESIDENTIAL ENERGY USE AND CONSERVATION--
UNITED STATES AND WESTERN EUROPE: SUMMARY

Eric Hirst
Oak Ridge National Laboratory

Historical Patterns of Residential Energy Use in the United States

Residential energy use increased steadily and rapidly from 1950 to 1972 at an average annual rate of 4 percent per year. Since then, energy use has been erratic and roughly static. Preliminary figures for 1976 shows a 5 percent increase over 1975. The distribution of fuels among the total changed significantly during this twenty-five year period. In particular, electricity's share increased markedly; this trend is likely to continue.

Until the early 1970s, real fuel prices declined smoothly for electricity and erratically for gas and oil. During the past few years, however, trends changed completely. All fuels now show increasing prices.

Space heating is the major fuel use in homes, accounting for about 53 percent of the total. Water heating accounts for another 14 percent. Refrigeration (refrigerators and freezers) add 8 percent. Air conditioning, which accounts for only 7 percent, is likely to show the greatest growth in the future because almost half the homes in the United States do not now have air conditioning.

Comparisons of Residential Energy Use in the United States and Western Europe

The determinants of household energy use are climate, housing type, house size, quality of construction, quantity of equipment/appliances, efficiency of equipment, and occupant behavior. Schipper   and

Lichtenberg's data show that although Sweden's winters are much more severe than those in the United States, Sweden uses only 75 percent as much energy per household as does the United States. Most of this is due to higher levels of insulation in Sweden; some is due to their greater propensity to live in multifamily units and smaller single-family units. Finally, they own fewer household appliances than do typical American households.

Residential use of energy relative to GDP rises more or less in line as income rises, but varies considerably according to energy prices paid by the residential sector.

Residential Energy Conservation Options in the United States

There are presently in existence cost effective conservation options in the United States residential sector. In a reference single-family house (built in accordance with the FHA MPS standards in effect in 1970), an extra investment of $600 would cut heating costs by more than 50 percent, relative to construction practices of the early 1970s. At today's gas price, this investment pays back in five years. The inclusion of air conditioning savings and the likelihood of higher gas prices in the future reduces the payback period.

A mobile home in Atlanta, Georgia, incorporating the 1975 HUD standards plus storm windows and additional insulation, would cut winter fuel bills by 50 percent at an extra cost of $400. The payback for this investment is six years.

Various design changes to a gas water heater reduce annual energy use, though at the cost of increasing purchase price. Energy use could be cut 24 percent with an increase in initial cost of 23 percent. The payback for this investment is three years. Our analyses show similar savings potential and short payback periods for electric water heaters and for refrigerators.

Alternative Projections of Residential
Energy Use in the United States

Four projections were developed with our engineering-economic model of residential energy use. In the high case, we assume that real fuel prices remain constant at their 1976 levels and that no government conservation programs are implemented. The baseline differs from the high case in that it includes rising fuel prices (from FEA's PIES model). The third case adds the residential conservation programs of President Carter's National Energy Plan. The final case includes much higher fuel prices after 1980 (50 percent increases over the FEA prices). Energy growth ranges from a high of 2.3 percent per year to a low of -0.1 percent per year (1976-2000). These are associated with varying levels of annual household energy-related expenditures (fuels and extra capital cost of improved equipment and structures). Cumulative economic effects of the residential conservation programs in the National Energy Plan indicate that (using a 8 percent real discount rate) fuel bill reductions are greater than higher capital costs by $27 billion. This suggests that conservation not only saves energy for the nation, but also saves money for households.

Conclusions

Comparisons of residential energy use in the United States and Europe show large conservation potentials.

1. The United States is now much more energy-intensive than is Europe.

2. Lots of options exist to reduce growth in the United States residential energy use--technological and behavioral.

3. European experience suggests that such changes need not cause "pain and suffering."

4. The United States residential energy use per household in 2000 could easily (and probably will) drop to today's European level.

PART IV

ENERGY POLICIES

UNITED STATES INTERNATIONAL
ENERGY POLICY: SUMMARY

William Milam
U.S. Department of State

The United States international policy is driven by the same basic
factors that drive domestic policies--dependence on a depletable resource,
oil.   International energy policy cannot substitute for the domestic programs
of the United States and other countries, but it can have some effect.   To
begin with, what is the situation with regard to the oil market?

What happens in the oil market depends almost totally on demand for
OPEC oil.   Given the one-shot increase in the supply of oil in the OECD countries from the Alaskan North Slope and the North Sea, there will be an easing
in the market over the next few years, but sometime in the early 1980's,
demand for OPEC oil will begin to press again on available supply, giving
upwards pressure on the real oil price in the market.

There are several variables in this scenario.   The most important one is
economic growth rates in the OECD.   Others include the impact of domestic
energy programs in the United States and other importing industrial countries,
and the success of the International Agency Exercise for Reduced Dependence,
which has a global target of keeping OECD demand for OPEC oil at about the
same level as it is now.   A further variable is the Socialist countries
demand for OPEC oil.   There is a good deal of disagreement in analytical
circles as to whether the Soviets and Eastern Europeans will be net importers
of oil by 1985 or not.

The other side of the energy policy question is the control that certain
members of the OPEC cartel have on the supply of oil in terms of political
embargoes.   Certain domestic and international programs have been established
to meet short-term supply disruptions of oil.   A further problem is the

impact that price rises would have on both short-term and long-term economic
stability in the OECD countries, and particularly on the economies of the
highly import dependent European countries and Japan.

The main thrust of the United States policy is to shift the supply curve
and demand curve for OPEC oil over time. First of all, there are programs
developed in the International Energy Agency. The IEA began as a response
to the embargoes and price rises of 1973 and 1974, and its first achievement
was the implementation of a major oil sharing program and the agreement among
participating countries to maintain emergency stocks of oil. At present each
country keeps about 70 days of emergency stocks, and this will rise to about
90 days in 1980. Beyond emergency programs to meet an embargo or other
supply disruption, the IEA has moved into a long-term program to reduce the
dependence on OPEC oil. The United States is also engaged through the IEA
in programs to develop new or alternative sources of energy and in an extensive R&D cooperation program in which countries are engaged in multilateral
efforts to develop alternative supplies of energy.

The United States also recognizes that there is a potential for increased
production of oil in some of the non-OPEC oil exporting less-developed countries, such as Mexico and Malaysia, but there is little to be done in terms of
international policy except to encourage these countries to move ahead as fast
as possible. Another potential source of oil is the reduction in imports by
currently oil importing developing countries: the United States has taken
some policy initiatives to increase the exploration and development of their
indigenous energy resources. The development requires substantially increased
capital flows to these countries as well as technical assistance in many cases.
Capital is inhibited in many ways from moving to these developing countries
in the amounts needed. The United States has initiated a new role for the
World Bank to act as a stimulant and catalyst for private flows by providing

front-end money into projects, either as a loan or an equity participation, and also by providing loans to governments for their own participation. With respect to the technology requirements for developing indigenous resources in LDCs, the United States has proposed an International Energy Institute which would be a multilateral organization to coordinate and to provide technical assistance to LDCs for energy development.

A final aspect of the United States' international energy policy is that towards OPEC itself. The United States policy in this regard has several thrusts. The United States is engaged in efforts to integrate OPEC economies more fully into the world economy and is also continuing diplomatic efforts to persuade OPEC members of the adverse effects of abrupt price rises on the economies of the industrialized countries and in particular on the economies of the less-developed countries. To the extent possible, the United States is also considering how to provide a climate for incentives for OPEC members who have the potential to produce more oil.

UNITED KINGDOM ENERGY POLICY: SUMMARY

Colin Brant
Energy Councilor, British Embassy

If the crisis of 1973 and 1974 was an inconvenience for the United
States, it was a disaster for the United Kingdom, both psychologically and
economically. By that time, the United Kingdom had become dependent for
half of its energy requirements on imported petroleum, much of it supplied
from countries affected by the renewal of Arab-Israeli hostilities. Consequently, the national security aspect of the crisis weighed very heavily.
On the economic side, the price rises of 1973/74 and later generated major
strains in the U.K. economy and greatly aggravated its balance-of-payments
problems.

Fortunately, with the development of North Sea oil and gas, this
prospect has been transformed. Since 1975, the fields in the North Sea have
come on-stream with gratifying regularity. By the end of this year, production should reach 900,000 to a million barrels of oil a day, which is well
over half of total internal demand. By the end of 1979 or the beginning
of 1980, North Sea production should be in balance with all domestic demand.

At the same time, other energy resources are not being neglected. The
United Kingdom is driving a four-fuels economy. For coal, for example, there
is a plan envisaging wholesale and thorough modernization of the coal industry by the year 2000. On the nuclear side, the advanced gas-cooled reactors
program is coming along well. The first units are now on-stream and in about
two or three years time, when all five reactors are in operation, 20 percent
of Britain's electricity will be generated by nuclear power. In addition,
Britain's prototype breeder reactor came on-stream some six months ago and
has since been feeding electricity into the national grid. The United Kingdom

must now face the decision of whether to go it alone for a large but expensive

commercial breeder reactor, say of 1,200 megawatts, or whether to look for

partners in a joint venture, sharing the increased costs involved. Finally,

the gas gathering system from the Frigg field should come on-stream next

month, bringing the first supplies of gas from this field of the Norwegian

section of the North Sea into the British gas distribution network.

Britain's principal policy problem is now how best to coordinate and

reconcile any differences among the four fuels to prevent any one fuel getting

out ahead of the others. We are seeking a flexible but robust policy that

can keep energy options open as far as possible. But there is one additional

point of policy: that the consumer should pay the real price of energy sup-

plies, reflecting the long-term supply costs of the fuel in question. This

avoids subsidization and should generate enough capital to maintain a strong

resource base, make necessary investments, and undertake innovative research.

The main exception to this rule so far has been in relation to gas, where the

British Gas Corporation is the monopoly purchaser. Their charter has hitherto

led them to operate on a cost-plus basis, with the resultant comparatively

low price being passed on to the consumer. This situation is changing as

British Gas buys its supplies from Norway at prices more reflective of world

levels.

The second major field of government decision is the adjustment of pro-

ducing and consuming facilities to achieve the balanced flexibility referred

to above. With oil, these decisions center on how fast the existing North

Sea fields should be depleted, at what rate fresh exploration licences should

be offered to the industry, whether associated gas should be flared or

reinjected, and the balance to be struck between refining at home and net

exports. With natural gas, the government's choices are how far and how fast

to promote extra gathering systems to bring incremental supplies from fields which would otherwise have gone untapped, and whether any fresh incentives to producers are needed.

With coal, the debate currently revolves on whether a coal-fired station should be brought forward to keep design teams in being with a view to exports later. In the nuclear field, there are two difficult decisions. First, what is our next generation of nuclear power plants to be--the advanced gas-cooled reactors which are proving successful at home or light water reactors which have export potential? And should Britain embark on a full-scale commercial breeder reactor, and if so, when?

A final point is that in the United Kingdom governmental decisions are made at different levels. The main vehicles of energy policy are state corporations which are entrusted with directing the national energy effort, but which are required to act on a commercial basis. At times, when they and the government take differing views of the national interest, this can lead to problems. On the other hand, policy formulation can be facilitated by this type of organization which permits relatively rapid decision making.

Conservation is regarded as an essential and integral part of overall energy policy and a vital element in the efficient use of resources. As already stated, fuel prices are to be set to reflect long-term supply cost. In addition, policies promoting cost-effective conservation practices have been instituted. Hitherto, the capital to undertake large-scale replacement of plant with more energy-efficient equipment has not been available, because of Britain's pressing economic difficulties. But now, with our balance-of-payments situation greatly improved, and the other main economic indicators favorable, we can consider plant replacement to achieve conservation as a more practical course.

ENERGY CONSERVATION IN THE OECD: PROGRESS AND RESULTS

Samuel A. Van Vactor*
International Energy Agency of the OECD

Introduction

As international co-operation on energy policy has progressed, there has
been a shift of emphasis and a changing perception of the problem. The oil
embargo of 1973-1974 caused immediate concern over the vulnerability of modern industrialized economies to disruption in energy supplies and sudden
price increases. There was less concern for the longer term implication of
the high level of dependence on oil and gas, resources of low cost and diminishing supply. However, attention has shifted and this has been accompanied by a generally less optimistic outlook for a reduction in international
oil prices and the availability of alternative energy supplies at reasonable
cost.

The shift of emphasis has important implications. Originally energy
conservation was conceived as a means to restore to consumers a measure of
control over the oil market; now it has a broader role. Energy conservation,
aiming at the wise and equitable use of low cost energy, is the key element
in programs intended to ease the transition to an economy based on scarcer
and more expensive energy supplies.

---

* The views expressed herein are his own and may not reflect the
official position of the Agency.

Development Since 1973

At the Washington Energy Conference of February 1974 and throughout the negotiations which led to the formation of the International Energy Agency (IEA), the United States insisted that "consumer co-operation" was a necesary prerequisite for its participation in a producer/consumer dialogue. Part of that co-operation was to include energy conservation.

Initially in the IEA negotiations, energy conservation was thought of as a tool with which to reduce oil imports and restore some measure of control over oil prices. For example, in January 1975 Secretary Kissinger remarked that the "objective conditions" for a reduction in the price of oil depended on:

> ... one, a degree of consumer solidarity that makes
> the consumer less vulnerable to the threat of embargo
> and to the dangers of financial collapse. Secondly,
> a systematic effort at energy conservation of sufficient
> magnitude to impose difficult choices on the producing
> countries. Thirdly, institutions of financial soli-
> darity so that individual countries are not so obsessed
> by their sense of importance that they are prepared to
> negotiate on the producers' terms. Fourth, and most
> important, to bring in alternative sources of energy as
> rapidly as possible so that the combination of new
> sources of energy creates a supply situation in which
> it will be increasingly difficult for the cartel to
> operate. We think the beginning of this will come
> within two to three years.[1]

---

[1] _Business Week_, January 1975.

With hindsight, it is obvious that Secretary Kissinger was highly
optimistic in his appraisal of future development of the oil market, but at
that time, the United States was experiencing the worst recession in recent
memory which had been accentuated by the increase in international oil prices.
Throughout the 1974-1975 period, the U.S. Government pursued a variety of
means in attempting to moderate or reduce oil price levels.[2]

Developments in the oil market, and the corresponding effect on the
perception of the future trend of oil prices, are critical to energy conservation. If the current real oil price level is viewed as a short term phe-
nomenon, to be readily corrected by the production of low cost alternative
supplies, then energy conservation could have a substantial cost to any
nation which vigorously pursued it. On the other hand, with permanently high
oil price levels, a delay in implementing energy conservation program might
retard economic growth.

Since the initial reaction by the U.S. Administration, the following
factors have worked to change the general perception of future oil price
movements:

- By winter 1975 OPEC oil production had fallen from its peak of 32
  million barrels per day to 25 million barrels per day. However,
  in 1976-1977, with economic recovery, production has surpassed
  1973 levels.

- Oil/gas reserve assessments, particularly in the United States,
  have been substantially reduced.

---

[2]Recent articles have suggested (for example, V. H. Oppenheim, "Why
Oil Prices Go Up--The Past: We Pushed Them Up," in Foreign Policy (Winter
1976/77)) that U.S. policy was not directed at reducing oil prices. The
present author who served as economist in the Energy Policy Office of the
U.S. Treasury from 1973-75 is unaware of any evidence that would support
this contention.

- Alternatives to oil and gas, such as oil shale and tar sands, appear to require a more advanced technology and are considerably more expensive than originally thought.

- In the United States, and many IEA countries, efforts to implement a strong energy program were initially frustrated.

- The above factors and other elements have been brought to the public's attention in a number of studies, including the OECD's World Energy Outlook, the CIA's The International Energy Situation: Outlook to 1985, and the MIT Energy Lab WAES Study.

The net effect of the accumulated information of the last four years has been to shift expectations with respect to future oil price movements. Consequently, energy conservation is becoming an increasingly attractive option. This is reflected in the development of programs in the IEA and the OECD.

In 1975 the IEA's main work in energy conservation was to set specific targets for oil imports, a two million barrel per day reduction.

In 1976 the IEA published Energy Conservation in the IEA, 1976 Review. This was the IEA's first publication and marks the emerging importance of energy conservation. The book contains an analysis of the different patterns of energy use among IEA members, a general survey of the levels of energy prices, an assessment of results, a brief description of the energy program in each country, and a list of recommended energy measures. The book has received a good deal of attention and has become the basis of further work in the IEA on energy conservation.

Future Developments

It is anticipated that many of the recommendations contained in Energy Conservation in the IEA will be elaborated and researched in some depth. To this end, a working group on Industrial Conservation is preparing a set of documents it hopes to publish next year.

The review of national energy conservation programs has now been integrated into an overall Energy Policy Review. This year seven countries, Japan, New Zealand, Norway, Greece, Canada, Luxembourg, and Austria have agreed to an in-depth examination of their policy. This examination will include a mission to the relevant capitals. Each mission will contain a conservation expert. In the case of Japan, the Chairman of the IEA's Conservation Group is the mission leader.

The IEA has a ministerial conference scheduled for this fall. It is anticipated that Ministers will agree on a set of energy conservation recommendations. These recommendations are likely to be on a par with those designed to encourage energy supply.

The IEA's R&D Committee is presently developing cooperative projects concerning:

- Energy conserving systems in building complexes
- Heat pumps
- Energy cascading
- Heat transfer and exchanges
- Improved combustion

It is anticipated that there will be many other R & D projects related to energy conservation.

The potential of co-operation in energy conservation remains large, partly because the principles of successful conservation programs are more

universally applicable to all nations, while the opportunities for supply
expansion vary enormously.

Two recent policy issues illustrate the importance of international co-
operation on energy conservation.

Canada has set special federal targets to move domestic oil prices
towards international levels, as an important means of encouraging energy
conservation. The pace of advancement is set, but subject to "safeguards."
Initially, federal policy sought to balance the concerns of consumers with
the need to encourage oil and gas exploration and development. Canadian oil
prices moved in a steady advancement to their present level, about $3.50
below the world oil price equivalent. At the current level they roughly
match the U.S. composite price of domestic and imported crude oil. Further
advancement of Canadian oil prices may now depend on the level of U.S. prices,
because if the Canadians were to set them higher, a number of Canadian
industries would be disadvantaged against their American competitors.

When President Carter announced his administration's energy policy, it
included proposed rebate on economy cars produced in the United States. It
was immediately clear that such a proposal would require negotiations with
other nations that exported cars to the American market. Otherwise, the
proposal could be construed as a barrier to trade.

Energy conservation policies can be inhibited by fears that they will be
competitively disadvantageous to home industries as well as fears that they
might be interpreted by allies as protectionism. In consequence, there is an
obvious need to co-ordinate the approach among trading partners.

The following policies from the IEA's recommended energy measures are
likely to have these sort of problems:

- Energy price levels, oil, gas, coal and electrical pricing to
  industry.

- Changes in electrical or natural gas price structures.

- Taxation of individual fuels.

- Energy labeling on appliances traded internationally.

- Mandatory efficiency requirements on appliances, cars, etc.

- Subsidies for energy conservation to industry.

There are other important reasons for international cooperation on energy conservation. With a couple of exceptions a higher growth rate of oil imports by an individual IEA country by itself would not contribute significantly to future imbalances of demand and supply. But, if each nation pursues policies aimed at **maximizing** short term benefits, it would precipitate a crisis very quickly. Cooperation on energy conservation policies must begin with a mutual appreciation of the energy problems. This in turn will make explanations to the general public easier. After all, the problem is international, and solutions are likely to require coordination. Government leaders may find that policies, such as energy conservation, which are designed to yield long term benefits, may have a lower political cost if the international burden is equitably shared.

Now we are taking first steps in energy conservation; devising energy conservation policies it is hoped will produce effects, as well as developing methodologies and means to learn from each other, how to copy success and avoid failure.

Summary and Evaluation of Energy Conservation Policies

In Energy Conservation in the IEA it was stated that:

- Conservation accomplishments and progress by IEA nations have been substantial.

- Nonetheless, significant potential still exists for reducing future energy demand in almost every country.

- The prospects for continued aggressive conservation thrust in many IEA nations are uncertain.[3]

Since then we have had a full year of energy policy developments. And, on balance, energy conservation has gained momentum. Broadly these accomplishments are as follows:

- Energy conservation is now the "cornerstone" of U.S. energy policy.

- Canada has made substantial progress in the last year and will, in most areas, match or exceed the U.S. program.

- France has developed an extensive program which seems to have produced considerable results.

- In the United Kingdom energy conservation programs have gained momentum and are an important part of the government's program.

- The Netherlands is in the process of developing a very substantial insulation program, and energy growth has been moderated.

- Japan, while relying to a large extent on market prices, has achieved considerable results.

- Germany, Italy, and Sweden already have programs in place but have initiated general energy policy reviews in which it is anticipated that energy conservation will gain an enhanced status.

The chart provided in How Industrial Societies Use Energy is a useful basis on which to judge the energy conservation program described in the preceeding section.[4]

---

[3]OECD, Energy Conservation in the IEA, p.7.

[4]Joel Darmstadter,Joy Dunkerley, Jack Alterman, How Industrial Societies Use Energy (Baltimore, Johns Hopkins University Press for Resources for the Future, 1977).

In the transportation sector, the United States and Canada are identified with significant potential for energy conservation. Both of these countries have lower gasoline taxes than the remaining countries. However, both Canada and the United States intend to mandate improved efficiency by requiring a higher mpg fleet average for new cars. In addition, almost all countries have indicated the desire to shift public funds generally from highway construction to public transport.

In the residential sector almost every country has some program to stimulate insulation and improved energy efficiency in buildings. Canada, the United States, and the Netherlands, three countries identified as having considerable potential in the residential sector, all have major insulation programs.

Energy conservation programs in the industrial sector have tended to rely on the market mechanism to a much larger extent. However, from 1973 to 1975 energy demand declined by 4.1 percent, and this is largely explained by a 10 percent decline in industrial demand. It is now too early to judge to what extent this is due to the recession. (Residential and transport energy demand remained approximately constant.) If industrial energy demand increases significantly in 1977 it will be clear evidence that additional programs are required.

The period since the oil embargo has been dominated by a major recession and continuing economic problems throughout the OECD. Overall GDP has increased by 4.1 percent, an annual rate of only 1.4 percent. Energy demand growth has been lower; preliminary figures indicate 1.1 percent, or an annual increase of 0.4 percent. Because energy demand has been lower than economic growth, the energy/GDP ratio has declined by 2.6 percent. These results raise several issues: to what extent does the experience since 1973 suggest that there is flexibility between economic growth and energy demand growth?

Secondly, how substantial is this result? Are our energy conservation
programs successful?

In Energy Conservation in the IEA, 1976 Review it was stated that " ...
the fact that countries with similar per economic output use very different
amounts of energy indicates flexibility of energy use, and thus conservation
potential."[5] Two major countries, Japan and France, which already have low
energy/GDP ratios have achieved very substantial results over the three year
period. In 1976 the United States, Japan, Germany, and France had the
highest economic growth rates of the countries surveyed in this article. All
but one of these countries have had a reduction in their energy/GDP ratio
greater than average. Since the 1973-1974 oil price increases there has not
been a "coupling" of energy demand and economic growth. If anything, the
opposite holds; most countries which have been successful in stimulating
economic recovery have managed also to reduce energy demand below where it
otherwise would have been. The fears often expressed about energy conserva-
tion--that it will result in a potentially lower standard of living--appear to
be unfounded.

Results, as hinted above, have been mixed. Not all countries have per-
formed the same manner each year over the three year period and in some
countries energy demand has grown faster than GDP. Overall, the 2.6 percent
reduction in the OECD's energy/GDP ratio, translates into a reduction in
energy demand the equivalent of 2 to 3 million barrels of oil per day. The
figure might, however, understate the actual energy savings. The period
1969 to 1972 is similar to the period 1973 to 1976. There was a recession
from the beginning of 1970 through 1971, although not as severe as the one

---

[5]OECD,   Energy Conservation in the IEA, p. 8.

in 1974 and 1975. From 1969 to 1972 the OECD energy/output ratio increased 1.9 percent. This is primarily due to a 3.8 percent increase in the United States. Without an oil price increase and energy conservation program the recent recession would likely have resulted in an increase in the energy/ GDP ratio rather than a decrease. Econometric analysis supports this observation. Also, it was a very cold winter. These factors may obfuscate energy conservation achievements.

Nonetheless, the present growth of energy demand reveals a disquieting trend. Quarterly data received at the OECD indicates that total primary energy demand increased by 6 percent in 1976 while economic output increased 5 percent. The same trend is evident in the annual data now being assembled. This in sharp contrast to the results in 1975, when there was a sharp decrease in energy demand relative to economic output. Results in 1976 have offset much of the 1975 gain. Consequently, the conservation programs in place cannot be judged unqualified successes. The potential for energy conservation is much greater, and existing programs have to be strengthened.

One final point remains. The most successful energy conservation plans surveyed in the following chapter use both administrative programs and the market mechanism to encourage energy conservation. Neither approach alone is likely to result in the optimum exploitation of the potential for energy savings.

Individual Country Programs

The United Kingdom

Conservation is regarded in the United Kingdom as an essential and integral part of overall energy policy. It is also seen as a vital element in the efficient use of resources, and the British Government has aimed at those detailed policies which are cost effective. In a July 1976 White Paper, the Department of Energy described the appropriate role for government in energy conservation.[6] That description is worth summarizing because it has universal application:

- Energy prices must reflect at least the costs of supply.

- Reinforced public awareness of the cost of energy and means of saving by providing clear and accurate information.

- Central governments and local authorities have a duty to set an example to the general public with respect to energy use in their own buildings and equipment.

- Public utilities and other fuel industries have wide scope to provide, as a service to customers, specialized advice and training on energy conservation.

- Research and development--particularly in areas where the incentives for private development are lessened because the full value of results may not be capture by the individual developer.

- The government should work to set technical standards, measurements and codes.

---

[6] Department of Energy, Energy Conservation, H. C. 487 (London, Her Majesty's Stationery Office, July 1976).

- Mandatory measures, for example, thermal insulation requirements
  for new buildings, providing there is the prospect for worthwhile
  economies.

In the United Kingdom energy conservation is complicated by the
prospect of considerable fuel switching with the continued growth of the
natural gas market.

From 1960 to 1973 demand grew more slowly than economic growth; the
ratio of TPE[7] to GDP actually fell by 10 percent. The government forecasts
the ratio to decline by an even greater amount by 1985.

The United Kingdom has the following programs in place:

- A high level ministerial committee on energy conservation designed
  to coordinate the government's role.

- A general publicity campaign, among the best financed in the OECD.

- Thermal insulation codes for new homes, roughly doubled in 1975.

- Efficiency standards for heating appliances; standards to be
  raised.

- Room temperature controls at 20°C for non-domestic buildings.

- Renovation grants for retrofitting existing homes with new
  insulation.

- Pilot studies on energy labelling.

- Job creation for unemployed youth in loft insulation.

- Energy savings targets by trade associations.

- Tax allowance for insulation--100 percent.

- An Energy Quick Advice service to answer questions by letter and
  telephone.

---

[7] Total Primary Energy Demand.

- A regional energy conservation liaison through the Department of Labor.

- An Energy Savings Loan scheme providing substantial funds for energy conservation investments.

- Development grants which could include combined heat and power.

- Energy Thrift Audit **and** Survey scheme designed to gather information to help firms and as a basis of policy decisions.

- Energy conservation seminars.

- Speed limits.

- A progressive vehicle tax in accordance with weight.

- Measures for car pooling under study.

- Consumption labels on cars by April 1978.

The United Kingdom government has explicitly stated that energy should be priced to cover at least the cost of supply. This statement was in response to a change of policy; in 1974 some energy supply industries had been subsidized as part of the government's anti-inflation campaigns. Not all energy is priced at replacement cost, however. This is particularly true for natural gas used in the domestic sector. Many energy commodities, for example, domestic natural gas, are priced below their counterparts in Europe. However, United Kingdom incomes lag behind many European incomes also, and this helps offset the lower prices. Gasoline is heavily taxed.

Energy Balances for the United Kingdom
(in mtoe)

	1973	1975	1976	1973-75 % Change	1973-76 % Change
Total Primary Energy Demand (TPE)	224.0	203.2	206.9	-9.3%	- 7.6%
TPE/GDP[a]	1.65	1.52	1.52	-7.9%	- 7.9%
Final consumption					
Industry	58.1	49.2	50.9	-15.3%	-12.3%
Transport	30.8	29.4	30.5	- 4.5%	- 1.0%
Others	53.8	52.0	52.2	- 3.3%	- 2.9%

[a]All TPE/GDP figures in this and other countries use mtoe (metric ton oil equivalent) for energy demand and 1970 U.S. dollars at 1970 exchange rates for GDP figures.

France

France was one of the first industrialized nations to take energy conservation seriously. The Agence pour les Economies d'Energie (Energy Conservation Agency) was established in November 1974, and from the very beginning aimed at reducing the long-term growth of energy demand. France's motivations for the early response were based on its policies and concerns, vis-a-vis OPEC and its own high level of oil import dependence, some 71 percent of total energy demand.

The Energy Conservation Agency has very broad authority to propose, research, and administer conservation programs. A very large proportion of its programs are mandatory, that is, they attempt to regulate lower energy consumption.

Energy consumption has been forecast at 285 mtoe for 1985, 5.5 percent annual growth. The government has set an apparently firm target of 240 mtoe, thus limiting demand growth to 3 percent per year from 1975, while holding 1974 and 1975 consumption below 1973 demand levels. So far, France has met its annual targets. The Energy Conservation Agency estimated that for 1976 13 mtoe have been saved, 7.5 percent. The most important savings have been in the residential/commercial sector, some 16 percent.

France has introduced the following measures since 1973:

- The Agency conducts energy conservation awareness campaigns and circulates information of new energy saving techniques.

- Detailed examinations by authorized experts of fuel burning and electrical equipment, with minimum standards now established.

- A special tax on the excess consumption of heavy fuel oil.

- Demonstration and subsidies for new techniques. (The subsidies can amount to as much as 50 percent of the cost.)

- New in 1977, interest rebates for loans on energy savings investment, with one billion francs allocated.

- Public information and education campaign.

- Control and distribution of domestic heating fuel.

- Temperature restrictions to 20°C for buildings, with fines for offenders.

- Rules on thermal insulation and ventilation.

- Income tax deductions for heat insulations and improvements.

- Restriction of display lighting.

- Appliance labelling.

- Restrictions on advertising which encourages energy consumption.

- Rearrangement of the pricing structure of heating and hot water to encourage conservation by final user.

- One third of all state housing improvement aid is now allocated for for purposes of insulation and other energy conservation projects.

- Free information on fuel efficiency and driving, and efficiency labels on new cars.

- Reduction of the VAT on urban public transport from 17.6 percent to 7 percent, offset by a gasoline tax increase.

- Improved traffic plans and revised public transport financing.

- R&D on motor design, and so forth.

In general, France prices energy products at levels which would correspond to the world market price. Electricity prices appear to be higher than average for countries with similar circumstances. Gasoline is heavily taxed.

Energy Balances for France
(in mtoe)

	1973	1975	1976	1973–75 % Change	1973–76 % Change
Total Primary Energy Demand (TPE)	183.7	168.1	177.9	− 8.5%	− 3.1%
TPE/GDP ratio	1.11	0.99	0.99	−10.8%	−10.8%
Final consumption					
Industry	55.0	49.2	52.4	−10.5%	− 4.7%
Transport	27.3	27.8	29.8	+ 1.8%	+ 9.1%
Others	54.8	47.6	49.6	−13.1%	− 9.5%

Japan

Japan is second only to the United States in levels of oil imports. Given continued economic growth and a successful American energy program, Japan is likely to soon emerge as the largest oil (or energy) importer in the industrialized world. Throughout the sixties oil imports to Japan grew at an annual rate of over 20 percent. This was accompanied by a growth rate of 13 percent in industrial production and 9.5 percent of GDP. All of these factors are combined with extremely limited domestic energy supplies. Obviously, a successful Japanese energy conservation program, one that moderates energy growth without endangering economic growth, is essential.

In a "Basic Direction of General Energy Policy" adopted in late 1975, the government set an energy saving target of 9.4 percent by 1985. In addition, Japan intends to discourage the development of energy intensive industries at home. The combination of these two policies is meant to have an overall savings of 16 percent.

Since 1973 Japan has introduced the following measures:

- A limited scheme to provide financial assistance for better thermal insulation.
- Mandatory efficiency improvements on freezers, refrigerators and air conditioners.
- Annual reports on fuel consumption by industry.
- Administrative guidance on fuel use.
- Rapid depreciation allowed for the installation of energy conservation equipment in small factories.
- Financial assistance by the Japan Development Bank for energy conservation.
- Speed limits.
- Preferential taxes and insurance rates for small cars.

●   Moderation of declining block rates.

●   Use of pumped storage to meet peak electrical demand.

In general, all energy is priced at world market levels. Gasoline is
heavily taxed. However, the price of kerosene for domestic space heating is
subsidized at the cost of other oil products.

Energy Balances for Japan
(in mtoe)

	1973	1975	1976	1973-75 % Change	1973-76 % Change
Total Primary Energy Demand (TPE)	337.8	331.9	349.3	-1.8%	+ 3.4%
TPE/GDP ratio	1.33	1.29	1.28	-3.0%	- 3.9%
Final consumption					
Industry	130.9	124.6	133.3	-4.8%	+ 1.8%
Transportation	39.7	41.4	43.2	+4.3%	+ 8.8%
Other	65.8	58.9	61.5	-10.5%	- 6.5%

The Netherlands

The rate of growth of energy demand, relative to economic growth, in the
Netherlands was the highest in the industrialized world prior to the 1973 oil
crisis. This is due to the importance of energy industries in the Dutch
economy as well as the development of the largest natural gas field in
Western Europe. Rotterdam is an oil import terminal and refinery center for
Germany, Belgium, and France as well as the Netherlands.

In 1973 the Dutch exported as much refined petroleum as they consumed. From 1968 to 1973 the chemical industries, especially fertilizers and petrochemicals, expanded at a very rapid rate. Overall, the industrial sector of energy consumption grew at 15 percent annual rate. The presence of abundant natural gas, at very cheap rates, contributed to this expansion.

The abundance of natural gas supplies had the largest impact in the residential sector. In 1965 only 10 percent of Dutch homes were centrally heated; now it is about 85 percent. Overall, in less than a decade, natural gas accounted for 50 percent of Dutch energy use.

From 1968 to 1973 the Dutch energy economic output elasticity was 1.8, that is, the ratio of energy demand growth to economic growth. For the future the Dutch Government forecasts that this elasticity will decline to 1.4 and, if additional measures are endorsed, to 1.2. Thus, energy conservation is meant to have a substantial impact on the Dutch economy and is an important part of industrial policy.

The Netherlands has introduced the following measures:

- Improved building codes for new residences built with state loans (most of these under construction). An improved standards through the Confederation of Dutch Municipalities for the remaining homes.

- A 33 percent grant to those retrofitting existing buildings with insulation.

- Voluntary energy labelling for household appliances.

- Other than the subsidy program for building insulation equally applicable to other sectors, no strong programs have been under-taken vis-a-vis industrial energy conservation. An information campaign was introduced late in 1976 and, of course, Dutch industrial policy is aimed at reducing energy intensive industries.

- The Netherlands have severe speed limits in place since 1973.

- There is a progressive tax on cars, by weight. Diesel cars and fuels are less heavily taxed than gasoline-fired cars and gasoline.

- Investment funds have been shifted from highway construction to public transport.

- Peak load pricing in the electrical industry is common and rates have been modified to reduce promotional pricing.

In general, Dutch energy prices are lower than those of other European countries. This is primarily because existing natural gas contracts have been honored. (This includes exports.) The Dutch are in the process of increasing the domestic price level, and petroleum products are priced at the world market equivalent. Gasoline, as in all European countries, is heavily taxed.

Energy Balances for the Netherlands
(in mtoe)

	1973	1975	1976	1973-75 % Change	1973-76 % Change
Total Primary Energy Demand (TPE)	61.7	59.0	65.2	-4.4%	+ 5.7%
TPE/GDP ratio	1.70	1.60	1.66	-5.9%	- 2.4%
Final consumption					
Industry	20.3	19.0	20.8	-6.4%	+ 2.5%
Transport	7.4	7.4	8.2	–	+10.8%
Others	20.4	20.6	22.0	+1.0%	+ 7.8%

Canada

Canada has a cold climate, low population density and high standard of living--all the factors which contribute to a high level of energy demand. Not surprisingly, energy use per capita is the highest in the OECD.

Energy conservation got off to somewhat a slow start. However, recently Canadians have taken a very active interest in its development. As a result, the Canadian conservation program is emerging as one of the better in the IEA. The federal government's goal is to reduce the average rate of energy demand to 3.5 percent from its historic levels of 5.5 percent.

The following measures are now in place:

- Fleet average performance standards for new cars to match the United States.

- Many provincial governments have adopted a 55 mph speed limit and the remainder are urged to.

- One hundred dollars surtax on car air conditioners.

- Graduated weight or fuel economy taxes for cars and station wagons from $30 to $300. Increases under consideration.

- Voluntary display of car fuel economy, which may become mandatory.

- Ten cent excise tax on gasoline by the federal government.

- A national federal home insulation grant program totalling $1.4 billion.

- Federal taxes on insulation and other energy saving equipment removed.

- Selected areas for home and factory energy audits and savings analysis.

- Voluntary energy conservation goals in twelve key industrial sectors.

- Information manuals and other programs for industrial energy conservation.

- Energy labelling for appliances.

- In-house federal government energy savings plan to cut energy use by 10 percent; includes new building code standards for federal buildings.

- More than 6 million energy conservation booklets have been distributed.

Energy Balances for Canada
(in mtoe)

	1973	1975	1976	1973-75 % Change	1973-76 % Change
Total Primary Energy Demand (TPE)	186.0	193.3	196.5	+3.9%	+ 5.6%
TPE/GDP ratio	1.86	1.87	1.81	+0.5%	- 2.7%
Final consumption					
Industry	40.2	37.2	41.1	-7.4%	+ 2.2%
Transport	33.9	36.7	37.8	+8.2%	+11.5%
Others	44.2	45.9	46.9	+3.8%	+ 6.1%

Germany

Germany is now in the process of a major review and revision of its energy policy. On March 22, 1977, the government issued a statement on energy targets. On the basis of this statement, it is clear that energy conservation will play a more important role than in previous plans. From 1960 to 1973 energy demand grew at about the same rate as GDP. The German government now anticipates this to change; from 1975 to 1985 they expect energy demand growth to be 90 percent of GDP growth. Following 1985, energy demand growth is expected to decline even more. These possibilities are borne out by the experience since 1973, where GDP has grown by 3 percent and energy demand by 2 percent. (However, these savings occurred in 1974 and 1975. From 1975 to 1976 energy demand grew by 11 percent while GDP grew by 6 percent.)

The emphasis on energy conservation represents a major shift of policy due to the increasing difficulty encountered in implementing Germany's nuclear program and the perhaps disturbing results in 1976. Until recently, the German Government had tended to rely exclusively on the price mechanism and was reluctant to intervene in specific end use sectors.

Germany has the following major conservation measures in place:

- A new law, as of July 1976, giving heat insulation standards for new buildings and standards for the installation, operation and maintenance of central heating systems.
- Temperature control and other measures in public buildings.
- A 7.5 percent investment allowance and other fiscal incentives, energy conservation investments.
- Grants for insulation and building modernization.
- A 1975 insulation retrofitting program.
- An education campaign and advisory body for smaller firms.
- Loans by the Reconstruction Loan Company to smaller firms.
- Use of gasoline tax revenue for public transport.
- Progressive vehicle tax by weight.
- Revision of electrical rate structures to moderate declining block rates and introduce peak load prices.

- A subsidy program to encourage 2.3 billion DM worth of district heating.

It is anticipated that the forthcoming government program will give retrofitting insulation in existing programs high priority, as well as additional fiscal measures for all areas of energy conservation.

Energy prices in Germany are at or above market levels for all fuels. The general energy price level is slightly above that of other European countries. Gasoline is heavily taxed.

Energy Balances for Germany
(in mtoe)

	1973	1975	1976	1973–75 % Change	1973–76 % Change
Total Primary Energy Demand (TPE)	265.8	243.5	260.5	−8.4%	− 2.0%
TPE/DGP ratio	1.26	1.19	1.20	−5.6%	− 4.5%
Final consumption					
Industry	82.8	72.7	73.8	−12.2%	−10.9%
Transportation	32.9	33.0	34.5	+3.0%	+ 4.9%
Other	78.7	70.8	77.2	−10.0%	− 1.9%

Italy

Energy use per capita is low in Italy; less than one half the IEA average. This is partially explained by the warm climate and a lower than average per capita GDP. Energy conservation is, nonetheless, very important because imported oil accounts for over two-thirds of the energy supply. The high level of expensive oil imports has created severe strains for the Italian economy.

Because per capita energy use is low, and so is energy use per unit of GDP, the Italian government believes that energy demand will grow at a higher rate than economic growth through the next decade. (This is a common belief among countries anticipating a high level of economic development.) Even though the energy/GDP ratio is likely to increase, it will not do so at its historic rate; from 1960 to 1973 the TPE/GDP ratio grew by 34 percent.

Italy announced a National Energy Plan in July 1975. Following the outline of the Plan, a unified bill on energy conservation was approved by the Chamber of Deputies in April 1976. The bill is primarily aimed at the residential sector. It is understood that the National Energy Plan is under study and may be revised. The revision is likely to prove an additional stimulus to energy conservation.

Italy has the following conservation measures in place:

- $20^{o}C$ established for existing heating systems.

- New thermal insulation standards for new and renovated buildings.

- A mandatory industrial data system which generates monthly reports on energy consumption by country.

- Progressive license fees based on number of cylinders and total displacement.

- Speed limits.

- Encouragement of public transport.

- Progressive electricity rates.

- A program under development for pumped storage.

- Programs to improve waste heat utilization.

In general, Italy prices energy at world market levels. There has been some criticism of electricity tariffs, but the average level appears to be above a number of other European countries. Gasoline is heavily taxed.

Energy Balances for Italy
(in mtoe)

	1973	1975	1976	1973-75 % Change	1973-76 % Change
Total Primary Energy Demand (TPE)	132.6	127.0	136.4	-4.2%	+ 2.8%
TPE/GDP ratio	1.28	1.23	1.24	-3.9%	- 3.1%
Final Consumption					
Industry	47.3	44.3	49.8	-4.3%	+ 5.2%
Transportation	19.6	19.2	18.3	-2.0%	- 6.6%
Other	32.1	32.6	36.5	+1.6%	+13.7%

Sweden

Sweden is most often cited as an example for the United States. Its standard of living is high, its population dispersed, and its climate cold, while its energy use is relatively low. In fact, its energy use per unit of GDP is one of the lowest in the IEA. This situation has not prevented Sweden from pursuing an active energy conservation program.

In 1975 the Swedish Riksdag adopted a resolution on energy policy. That resolution contains a commitment to "deliberate conservation." The basis for this policy is concern for the environment and an ultimate question of management of the earth's resources. The Swedish government aims to reduce energy demand growth from its historic rate of 4.5 percent to 2 percent through the 1985 period. Beyond 1990 they aim to hold energy consumption at a constant level. In order to accomplish this objective, the Swedish government desired to establish "a form of preparedness whereby we can rapidly intervene should developments take a different course from that which we are now seeking to follow."

Since 1975 there has been a change of government. One of the issues in the campaign was the use of nuclear energy for electrical power generation. The present Prime Minister promised to downgrade the use of nuclear power if elected.

It was intended, when the 1975 plan was approved, that proposals for the period following 1985 would be put before the Riksdag in 1978. To this end an Energy Commission has been established. The Commission will draw on the previous plan and present experiences. It is anticipated the new plan will rely heavily on energy conservation. The new government intends to introduce a program to improve energy efficiency in home heating and power, and incentives to utilize waste heat.

Sweden has the following energy conservation measures in place:

- New building codes with strict energy efficiency standards for new and renovated buildings.

- A program of public information on energy conservation.

- Individual metering for electricity and hot water.

- Loans and grants for energy conservation in existing buildings. Extended and improved in 1976.

- Government control concerning the establishment of energy intensive industries, and their energy use designs.

- Forthcoming legislation on municipal energy planning.

- State grants (up to 35 percent) for energy conservation in industrial buildings, and processes. Fifty percent grants for prototype and demonstration projects. Extended in 1976.

- Studies underway on industrial conservation potential.

- Progressive taxation on cars.

- Speed limits.

- Wide use of district heating and continued expansion.

- Peak load pricing and electrical exchanges with Norway, Finland, and Denmark.

- Construction of cogeneration plants.

- R&D in energy conservation.

- Increased taxes on petrol, LP gas, oil, coal, coke, and electricity.

In general, energy prices in Sweden are at world market levels. Electricity prices, because of abundant hydro power, are generally below other European countries. Gasoline is heavily taxed.

Energy Balances for Sweden
(in mtoe)

	1973	1975	1976	1973-75 % Change	1973-76 % Change
Total Primary Energy Demand (TPE)	47.1	47.2	50.3	0.2%	+ 6.8%
TPE/GDP ratio	1.34	1.28	1.34	-4.5%	-
Final consumption					
Industry	15.7	15.2	15.4	-3.2%	- 1.9%
Transportation	5.2	5.5	5.7	+5.8%	+ 9.6%
Other	14.1	13.4	14.9	-5.0%	+ 5.7%

The United States

From 1960 to 1973 oil consumption grew at 7.1 percent annual rate in Europe, 18 percent in Japan and 3.9 percent in the United States. In all three areas total energy demand grew at about the same rate as economic output. Why then is energy conservation so important for the United States? There are three reasons. Energy use in the United States was much higher than most other countries in 1960, thus even modest energy demand growth in the United States has a major impact. Secondly, the rate of increase of U.S. oil production slowed and then peaked in 1970; likewise, natural gas peaked in 1973. Since then, there has been a steady decline of domestic supplies in both products. This translated into an unprecedented increase in oil imports; 17.4 percent in 1971, 20.6 percent in 1972, and 30.4 percent in 1973. A continuation of such a trend would have profound and undesirable consequences in the international oil market in terms of its impact on price as well as precipitating potential shortages. Thirdly, oil consumption grew at a very high rate in Japan and Europe, because it was replacing coal and other fuels. This substitution is now more or less complete. In the United States however, given the growing scarcity of low cost energy supplies, additional energy demand is likely to translate directly into additional oil imports.

Fortunately President Carter and Congress have recognized the seriousness of the situation. Energy conservation has been made the "cornerstone" of the U.S.'s National Energy Plan, and a major effort towards reversing historic trends appears to be underway.

From 1973 through to 1976 the United States introduced the following energy conservation measures:

- Some state building codes which take account of energy efficiency.
- Mandatory energy labelling for major house appliances.

- Energy efficiency targets for appliances to achieve a 20 percent improvement by 1980.

- An in-house federal government energy conservation program which resulted in a 24 percent savings.

- A federally funded program to stimulate state energy conservation.

- Voluntary energy conservation targets by 1980 in industry.

- Mandatory fleet average fuel economy standards for new cars, 20 mpg by 1980 and 27.5 mpg by 1985.

- Speed limits at 55 mph on all roads.

- Increase in public transport spending. Diversion of Federal Highway Trust Fund to maintenance as well as capital expenditure.

- Encouragement of car and van pooling.

- "Automatic cost pass-through" for fuel used in many electrical utilities.

- Federal funding of electrical rate demonstration projects.

- Low income residential conservation program.

In April President Carter proposed the following measures, and it appears that Congress will approve a high proportion of the President's Plan:

- A "gas guzzler" tax and rebate on efficient cars.

- Reaffirmation of the fleet average fuel economy standard of 27.5 mpg for 1985.

- Standby gasoline tax.

- Efficiency standards for light duty trucks.

- Removal of 10 percent excise tax on intercity buses.

- Adjustment of taxes on aviation and marine fuel.

- Federal programs in van pooling and auto purchasing practices.

- A national residential energy conservation program for existing building to include; tax credits on insulation, local utility

financing, FHA loans, expansion of low income residential conservation program, rural home weatherization, and federal grants
to non-profit organizations.

- Mandatory efficiency standards for new buildings.

- Improvement of old federal buildings by 20 percent and new ones by
  45 percent.

- Mandatory, rather than voluntary, appliance targets.

- An additional 10 percent investment tax credit for industry.

- A program to develop the cogeneration of electricity and process
  heat.

- A demonstration program and encouragement of district heating.

- Utility rate reform to include: a phasing out of promotional
  electricity and gas rates, introduction of peak load pricing,
  individual metering requirements, and improved interconnection
  of electrical grids.

- Oil and natural gas taxes to bring these fuels to the world
  market level.

Energy pricing in the United States has, of course, been a highly
contentious issue. In its review of the U.S. conservation program, the IEA
identified U.S. energy pricing policy as the single most critical issue
governing the prospect for reduced oil imports. It has been the judgment of
the IEA review process that U.S. oil and gas prices equivalent to the world
price level is a necessary prerequisite for a successful energy conservation
program. Currently, oil and gas prices are, on average, below the world
equivalent. In addition, due to the various regulatory programs, final
consumption prices vary enormously. This has caused a large number of

distortions, for example, gas use in electricity generation, refineries and the industrial sector is double that of Europe.[8] (President Carter's proposed program will go a long way towards resolving many of these problems.) Gasoline is not heavily taxed in the United States. However, the program to improve car efficiency should offset, in part, this energy conservation disadvantage.

Energy Balances for the United States
(in mtoe)

	1973	1975	1976	1973-75 % Change	1973-76 % Change
Total Primary Energy Demand (TPE)	1727.4	1651.0	1743.9	− 4. 4%	+ 0.9%
TPE/GDP ratio	1.54	1.51	1.51	− 1.9%	− 1.9%
Final consumption					
Industry	402.0	350.9	357.9	−12.7%	−11.0%
Transportation	406.5	412.2	425.8	+ 1.4%	4.7%
Other	431.0	408.0	461.7	− 5.3%	7.1%

From 1973 to 1975, while it has grown in Europe, the use of gas in refineries declined substantially but it is still over half the energy used compared to negligible use in Europe.

---

[8]To some extent this reflects supply opportunities. The use of natural gas in these sectors did decline slightly.

PART V

CONCLUSIONS

THE USES AND LIMITATIONS OF INTERNATIONAL
ENERGY CONSUMPTION COMPARISONS

Lincoln Gordon
Resources for the Future

The following series of current quotations suggests the wide range of

opinions on the significance of international energy consumption comparisons.

1. Jimmy Carter: "Germany, Sweden, Japan and other countries
    have the same standard of living as we do, as far as the
    material things are concerned. They use only one half
    as much energy as we do. So I think we need to cut back
    on the consumption and waste of energy. That is the main
    thing to do."[1]

2. Denis Hayes: "International comparisons support the con-
    tention that the 1975 U.S. energy budget can be trimmed
    over time by more than one-half. For example, Sweden,
    West Germany and Switzerland, with about the same level
    of per capita GNP as the United States, use only 60 percent
    as much energy per capita as does the United States."[2]

3. Chauncey Starr and Stanford Field (EPRI): "As this study
    shows, the argument that the United States has a low average
    GDP/E (Gross Domestic Product to Energy) ratio when compared
    to other nations, and is therefore energy inefficient, is
    both simplistic and misleading. One cannot characterize
    the proficiency of a society's resource use by considering
    only one of the input variables (i.e., capital, labor,
    materials, or energy). The more significant measure of
    proficiency is how successfully all these inputs are inte-
    grated to establish national well-being."[3]

4. Lee Schipper and Allan J. Lichtenberg: "Thus, international
    energy use comparisons, far from suggesting an inevitable
    coupling between level of economic activity and energy use,

---

[1]President Carter, replying to a question at the "Town Meeting" at
Yazoo City, Mississippi, July 21, 1977.

[2]Denis Hayes, Energy: The Case for Conservation, Worldwatch Paper 4,
Washington, Worldwatch Institute, January 1976) p. 14.

[3]Chauncey Starr and Stanford Field, Energy Use Proficiency: The
Validity of Inter-Regional Comparisons (Palo Alto, California, Electric
Power Research Institute, March 1977) p. 14.

actually suggest ways in which more well-being can be wrought from every Btu of fuel and kilowatt-hour of electricity consumed in a given country."[4]

5. Henry R. Linden: "I think it is safe to say that we do not yet know how to go about uncoupling energy consumption from GNP. Consequently, conservation is much too benign a label for this policy option in the near term. Rather, it should be presented to the public as what it likely will be for the foreseeable future: a policy of lower real income, reduced standard of living, reduced mobility, and, possibly, higher unemployment.... There are countries with high standards of living...which have a lower energy consumption to GNP ratio than the US... However, these are countries in which the economy depends largely on high-value goods and services.... Thus, the value of this parameter seems to depend primarily on the particular mix of economic activity and possibly also on such factors as population density and climate, rather than on the relative costs of energy or relatively minor cultural differences such as those between highly-developed western nations."[5]

6. Joel Darmstadter, Joy Dunkerley, and Jack Alterman (RFF): "Why is per capita consumption of primary energy resources so much higher in the United States than it is in other advanced industrial countries--such as Sweden, Germany, and France--whose per capita income does not differ appreciably from that of the United States? The importance of the issue is clear enough. If the answer to the question points to the possibility that the American standard of living can be maintained at a much lower level of energy use, such a finding could have major significance for the direction and eventual payoff from conservation strategies that the United States might see fit to undertake."[6]

I. The Advocacy Role of International Comparisons

The quotations also illustrate the dual operational role of international comparisons. On the one hand, such comparisons can be used as support for a

---

[4] Lee Schipper and Allan J. Lichtenberg, "Efficient Energy Use and Well-Being: The Swedish Example," Science vol. 194, no. 4269 (December 3, 1976) pp. 1001-1013, at p. 1012.

[5] Testimony by H. R. Linden, President, Institute of Gas Technology, at Public Seminar, Energy Policy and Resource Development, President's Energy Resources Council, December 10, 1974, Department of State, Washington, D.C., pp. 2-3.

[6] Joel Darmstadter, Joy Dunkerley, and Jack Alterman, How Industrial Societies Use Energy: A Comparative Analysis, Preliminary Report, (Baltimore, Johns Hopkins University Press for Resources for the Future, 1977) p. 1.

position arrived at independently--the _advocacy role_. On the other hand,
they can be used to provide illumination and guidance concerning the array
of energy options--the _policy role_. There may also be a non-operational
role. All comparative studies (whether historical or cross-sectional) help
to sharpen perceptions of any culture by reminding the scholar and the reader
that their own are not the only possible ways of life. This workshop, however,
is presumably focused on the operational roles.

The more simplistic advocacy uses of international energy consumption
comparisons bring to mind Shakespeare's comment on the flexibility of
scriptural citations. President Carter and Mr. Hayes are seeking to leave
their audience with the impression that a 40 or 50 percent difference in
per capita energy use _ipso_ _facto_ demonstrates that 40 or 50 percent of
America's energy consumption is pure waste. Mr. Linden (and similar observations in the Chase Bank energy studies) is seeking to leave the impression
that any reduction in per capita energy consumption necessitates a corresponding
reduction in overall production, incomes, welfare, and employment. Somewhat
surprisingly, in spite of its committed advocacy, the Ford Foundation Energy
Policy Project made only a passing reference to international comparisons,
perhaps out of concern that more detailed examination might create more doubts
than support for the preferred goal of zero energy growth.[7]

As any trial lawyer will confirm, the arguments of advocacy need not
always meet rigorous tests of logical coherence and factual objectivity.
In an open society, however, as in an open courtroom, adversary procedures
push the arguments in that direction. Adversary proceedings are not the
only way of seeking truth. For purposes of scientific investigation they
are generally not the best way. In our own society, fortunately, many

---

[7]_A Time to Choose_, Final Report by the Energy Policy Project
of the Ford Foundation (Cambridge, Massachusetts, Ballinger, 1974) p. 6.

scholarly institutions have survived the assault of the new intellectual
nihilists, who preach that social science cannot be objective and that the
only criterion for an argument's validity is its political worth as an
instrument of power. Resources for the Future is one of those institutions.
Hence, this workshop.

We are confronted with two kinds of issues. (1) Do international
consumption comparisons provide valid illumination and guidance on relevant
energy policy options? (2) If so, in what ways are they useful for policy
making and in what ways mere curiosities or irrelevant deflectors of attention?

II. The Validity of International Comparisons

In this context, "validity" of comparisons means that like is being
compared with like, or that elements of difference are systematically
distinguished from elements of similarity, or that the causes of the
differences are systematically accounted for. No two national societies
are identical in all respects; if they were, nothing could be learned from
comparing them. Our interest is in sets of differences that bear on particular
aspects of American energy policy: (1) the possibilities of reducing energy
consumption without parallel reductions in welfare or substantial changes
in lifestyle; (2) the kinds of changes in lifestyle which might further
reduce energy consumption without parallel reductions in welfare; and (3) the
kinds of instruments, such as changes in price levels or price structures,
institutional reforms, incentives and penalties, or other forms of intervention
which might bring about desired reductions in energy consumption at lowest
net cost to the society.

Underlying these three objectives is the assumption that energy conservation is desirable if it _can_ be secured without parallel reductions in
welfare. In view of the price increases since 1972, the prospect of further
increases, the fact that for many years to come the politically unstable

Middle East will be the source of marginal supplies, and the enormous difficulties of the long-term transition away from oil and gas as major energy sources, that assumption seems almost self-evident. It can be argued on the merits if necessary.

Setting aside any element of pure advocacy, Linden and (to a lesser extent) the EPRI team are arguing that differences of economic structure make international comparisons among advanced industrial countries invalid or irrelevant, while the RFF team, Schipper, and the other country studies[8] work on the premise that the effects of structural differences can be sufficiently isolated to make comparisons valid in the sense defined above. One potentially distracting element in all international economic comparisons, the selection of appropriate currency exchange rates, has fortunately been removed by the Kravis studies of purchasing power parities, which are used by RFF and the bilateral country studies and acknowledged by EPRI, but not yet recognized by Linden.[9] That leaves the large issue of whether structural differences (in the proportions of economic activities with varying degrees of energy intensity per unit of output) account for all differences in consumption, thus rendering comparisons almost useless, or whether structure and

---

[8] In addition to the Schipper-Lichtenberg study of Sweden cited in footnote 4 above, detailed bilateral comparisons of energy consumption between the United States and West Germany and Japan are now available. For Germany, see the paper by Richard L. Goen and Ronald K. White, Comparison of Energy Consumption Between West Germany and the United States, prepared for the Federal Energy Administration (Menlo Park, California, Stanford Research Institute, June 1975) and summarized in Ronald K. White's contribution to this workshop. For Japan, see the paper for this workshop by Andres Doernberg on "Energy Use in Japan and the United States." Although they differ in degrees of disaggregation and other details, their general approaches and methodologies are similar and their authors support the view that international comparisons are both feasible and useful.

[9] Irving G. Kravis et al., A System of International Comparisons of Gross Product and Purchasing Power (Baltimore, Johns Hopkins University Press for Resources for the Future, 1975). See Henry Linden, Institute of Gas Technology, "Perspectives on US and World Energy Problems" (unpublished paper, October 1, 1976) p. 3.

intensity can be validly sorted out. In this connection, structure refers
not only to the distribution of production among broad economic sectors and
particular industries and specialties within sectors, but also the geographical
environment and the locational patterns of economic activities and distribution
of population.

The Starr-Field paper has done yeoman service in analyzing the inter-
relationships among energy use, economic activity, and labor productivity on
a state-by-state basis within the United States. They demonstrate dramatically
the effects of differing economic structures on energy use per capita, even
where gross product per capita is fairly well clustered and output per employed
worker even more so. Louisiana's use of energy per unit of product (in 1971)
was more than five times that of Connecticut, even though per capita income
in Connecticut was 50 percent higher than Louisiana. (That does _not_ demonstrate, by the way, as some advocates might suggest, that low energy
consumption is a recipe for securing affluence!)[10]

Where one must seriously question the Starr-Field analysis is their
assumption that industrial countries differ from one another as much as or
more than our several states. Their own data for nine countries (p. 11)
show an intercountry range of only 2:1 in energy consumption per unit of
product, compared with 5:1 among the states. That is not surprising, since
national policies in all but the smallest countries tend to favor "balanced"
economic development, which implies greater self-sufficiency in food supplies
and a more representative array of heavy and light industries and service

---

[10]There are technical deficiencies in the Starr-Field method of calculating
Gross State Product by applying proportions of state personal income to national
personal income, since some of the income in states of high wealth is generated
in other states. To correct these deficiencies, there would be required state-
by-state trade and balance-of-payments data, which do not exist. However,
this point does not detract from the central thrust of the argument.

activities than would be located there under conditions of total international

mobility for goods, labor, and capital.

Having overstated the differences inherent in intercountry comparisons,

Starr and Field go on (pp. 11-12):

> Does a comparison of the GDP/E ratio of France with that
> of the U.S. mean that France is using energy twice as
> effectively as the U.S. in the production of goods and
> services?--not likely. As indicated earlier, the reasons
> for the differences in GDP/E ratios are to be found in the
> differences attributable to such variables as national
> resource endowments, geography and climate, population
> density, living styles, relative cost of energy, economic
> history and structure, social values and criteria and the
> mix of agricultural, industrial and service activities.

They are certainly correct in emphasizing the importance of resource endowments,

geography, population density, and the mix of economic activities--the typical

structural elements which account for an important share of international

differences in energy consumption. They are also correct in pointing out

that energy is applied jointly with other factors of production (labor,

capital, and other materials), and the "effectiveness" of energy use in

production cannot be judged without taking into account the costs of those

other factors, all of which are to some extent substitutable for and by

energy. But if the purpose of the comparisons is to provide guidance on

realistic conservation possibilities under the changed circumstances of

higher energy costs and greater insecurity of energy supplies, then differences

in living styles, relative cost of energy, economic history, and social values

and criteria may point directly to fruitful lines of conservation policy.

These elements are typically the sources of differences in intensity of energy

use.

Failure to recognize the distinction between structure and intensity

can easily lead to the blind alley of arguing that history and tastes have

created incommensurables, to the point where there can be no such thing as

a valid comparison of energy efficiency. The extreme reductio ad absurdum of that line of thought would be to argue that if X sets his thermostat at 80° and opens his windows to avoid overheating, no energy waste is involved because conspicuous consumption must rate high on X's schedule of personal preferences! Dr. Starr's paper for this workshop, far from embracing that line, moves closer to the position taken here.

The RFF team and the bilateral country studies are not claiming that differences in energy usage are purely arbitrary, without historical or rational explanation. They are claiming that the effects of structural differences can be separated (in large measure, if not completely) from those of energy intensity. Relative cost of energy is a different issue, since a central purpose of policy-oriented international comparisons is to seek guidance on more efficient energy use from the experience of countries which have long faced the higher levels of energy cost which are a novelty to Americans.[11]

Since consumption patterns of modern industrial countries are much more similar than production patterns, differences in energy consumption resulting from differing structures of production can in theory be compensated by determining the embodied energy exported or imported in goods and services crossing national frontiers. (At the state level, likewise, while no comprehensive data are available, it is obvious that a state such as Louisiana exports much more embodied energy than it imports.) To make that determination accurately would require an inordinately refined breakdown of categories, and

---

[11]The Starr-Field paper correctly criticizes Schipper for measuring hydroelectric and nuclear power inputs to manufacturing on a net basis rather than a fuel-equivalent basis (for electricity generated from fossil fuels). The RFF team converts all "primary" electricity into fuel equivalents. As brought out during the workshop proceedings, different forms of energy give rise to differences in efficiency of combustion (or other application), so that a finely structured comparative study would have to allow for such differences as they affect each sector or industry. At the level of aggregation in the studies reviewed here, however, the "primary energy equivalent" is a less distorting measure than the net energy contained in electricity generated by hydro or nuclear power.

also of sources of imported goods. Without trying the impossible, the RFF

team and the country studies have made sufficient approximations of net

embodied energy movements to feel satisfied that they do not contradict

findings based on more practicable sources of data.

On the central issue of whether valid and meaningful international

comparisons of energy consumption are possible, therefore, the balance of

judgment should be favorable. Unless the elements of structure and intensity

are sorted out as far as analysis makes possible, however, international

comparisons can be seriously misleading.

There is a further weakness of cross-sectional studies limited to a

single year, a point noted briefly in the RFF study (p. 30). They provide

no light on the stability of differences in energy intensity, and whether

those differences are growing or diminishing. The indications of convergence

in GDP/E ratios are tantalizing, making one wonder whether the Americanization

(or what our European critics used to call "cocacolonization") of consumption

patterns in all affluent countries is just a matter of time. The "automobili-

zation" of Western Europe and Japan (and its incipient thrust into Eastern

Europe), notwithstanding high fuel prices, inadequate roads, and urban

traffic congestion, seems to point in that direction. Sector-by-sector

analyses combining time series and international comparisons would add sub-

stantially to the illumination provided by single year snapshots. They would

also assist in estimating medium- and long-term demand elasticities for energy,

which logic tells us must be far higher than short-term elasticities.

III. The Policy Role of International Comparisons

Having satisfied ourselves that valid international comparisons are

feasible, we must still ask whether and in what ways they are useful for

policy making. Five types of potential usefulness come to mind.

A. <u>The Heuristic Role</u>. At a minimum, serious international comparisons are thought-provoking, demonstrating that there can be differing degrees of energy intensity for given levels of output, pointing toward the sectors with the largest opportunities for conservation, and suggesting what methods of conservation might least impinge on levels of welfare or entrenched life-styles. At the same time, they should help to decontaminate the policy debate by unveiling the simplism of the gross comparisons often used in the heat of advocacy.

This heuristic role is indicative and qualitative, rather than precise and quantitative. It must evidently be supplemented by analyses dealing directly with specific American conditions. In a memorandum on the draft of the RFF study last December, I commented that it "points toward the conclusion that higher energy efficiency in passenger transport, in residential space conditioning, and in some industrial applications provide opportunities for substantial energy saving in the U.S. without radical changes in life-styles or locational patterns." The counter argument can be made that the same conclusions would emerge from a sector-by-sector study of U.S. energy use, without benefit of international comparisons. Whether rational or not, however, it is a fact that such conclusions are more persuasive if they can be backed by real world experience in fairly similar environments.

The heuristic role is analogous to the celebrated blow with a 2x4 to gain the mule's attention. The usefulness for policy does not end there.

B. <u>Demonstration of Demand Elasticities</u>. Most other industrial countries have had years of experience with higher energy costs and prices than the United States. The differentials in our favor resulted from low-cost domestic supplies: first coal and hydropower; later oil; and then gas in the period since World War II. It is true that, for a couple of decades, our import restrictions led to domestic crude oil prices above world market levels, but for products at retail, notably gasoline, high excise taxes in other countries much more than made up for this differential. Thus a series of laboratories are available for examining the effects of different price levels. They are admittedly not clean laboratories, and they do not permit the kind of controlled experimentation one expects in the physical sciences. Nevertheless, actual experience abroad over many years with price levels similar to those soon to face the United States is surely superior to the extrapolations in some studies, especially of gasoline consumption, based on very small and often short-lived price differentials among our own states or cities.

C. <u>Methods of Energy Conservation</u>. Behind the effects of higher prices as measured in energy demand elasticities lies the question of how those effects were achieved. In the industrial and commercial sectors, where economic efficiency may be expected to dominate, a mixture of alternative technologies and business practices will normally account for lower inputs of energy per physical or value unit of output. Clearly some kind of factor substitution is at work here; even examples of apparent "pure waste," like open factory doors in cold weather, probably have some offset in added convenience or lower labor costs. But when a sharp increase in relative energy costs takes place, knowledge of foreign experience can accelerate the indicated adjustments and international comparisons can guide policy makers on the probable magnitudes of feasible energy savings.

The response of households is more conjectural, since tastes, habits, and lifestyles are involved along with economic motivations. Even there, however, international comparisons have some relevance, both as guides to workable policies and as warnings against unrealistic ones.

D. __Institutional Arrangements and Methods of Governmental Intervention__.
In some of the sectors with largest apparent potential for energy conservation,
a combination of price incentives with regulatory or institutional interventions
seems to promise optimum results. Some of the interventions may work through
the price mechanism, such as energy excise taxes, automobile horsepower
taxes, or required alterations in electricity rate structures. Others will
operate directly, such as automobile mileage requirements or minimum insulation
standards for buildings. Still others may involve institutional reforms,
such as arrangements for district heating from power plants or linkage of
industry-owned generators to public utility systems. In all these cases,
systematic reviews of international experiences can provide guidance on
relative effectiveness of alternative policy combinations and on unsuspected
pitfalls which may trap the unwary policy maker. In these matters, it is
always useful to keep in mind a Brazilian maxim: "In practice, the theory
is different."

E. __International Policy Making__. The program of energy policy cooperation
among the principal industrial countries worked out through the OECD's International Energy Agency includes an emergency oil import sharing agreement
to be triggered by 7 percent reductions in oil supplies to the group as a
whole or to any one of its members. The purpose is to forestall the possibility
of selective oil embargoes like those imposed by the Arab members of OPEC
against the United States and the Netherlands in 1973/74. There are also
longer-term commitments to "rational use of energy," and arrangements for
annual reviews of energy conservation in IEA countries.[12]

---

[12] A summary of the program appears in the OECD Observer, no. 73, January-
February 1975, pp. 20-25. The results of the first annual review are in
Energy Conservation in the International Energy Agency: 1976 Review (Paris,
OECD, 1976).

The emergency sharing agreement does not call for identical conservation measures in advance, although once an emergency is declared all the members are obligated to reduce oil consumption by the same percentages. As a practical matter, however, the political viability of the arrangement in the face of any extended embargo or other supply emergency (which might result from sabotage, accident, or localized hostilities in a major supply area such as the Persian Gulf) would be badly undermined by glaring differences in seeming "wastefulness." In those conditions, international cooperation would encounter a good deal of recrimination, and might easily break down completely. Well-based international consumption comparisons, especially if conducted by multinational teams under international auspices, could help to minimize unwarranted recriminations and facilitate international collaboration for both emergency and longer term purposes.

*   *   *   *

These observations suggest a considerable range of policy usefulness in serious international comparative energy consumption studies. It should be noted that the main applications are at the sectoral and sub-sectoral levels, where structural and intensity components can be more fully sorted out and where policy measures must be applied. The workshop papers and discussions have made eminently clear that the validity of international comparisons is almost directly proportional to the degree of disaggregation, and that the methodology of comparative studies should be related to the specific purpose of the comparisons.

It should not be supposed, however, that valid international comparisons will free the policy debates from controversy. In addition to conflicts generated by the clash of direct and indirect economic interests, disputes will arise from the absence of any purely objective definition of what constitutes a significant change in lifestyle, to say nothing of disagreements on what changes are acceptable or desirable. In my own judgment, for example,

industrial and commercial energy conservation and better insulated housing
have no effect on lifestyles; somewhat lighter and smaller automobiles, car
pooling, returnable containers, more conservative lighting standards, and
thermostat settings of 68–70° in winter and 78–80° in summer (instead of
vice versa) have only minor effects; but shifts to mass transit commuting,
dwelling in urban apartments instead of suburban houses, or keeping only
the kitchen warm in winter would constitute substantial changes which would
face severe public resistance. The judgments of others might be quite different.

The most serious potential abuse of international consumption comparisons
would be to generate complacency about the ease of achieving major conservation
results or to bolster the erroneous (and quite widespread) notion that conservation alone can constitute an adequate energy policy. Even with zero
energy growth, alternative supplies would be needed to replace the dwindling
output from established oil and gas fields. There is also good reason to
believe that conservation simply lowers the slope of the growth path for a
couple of decades, while the capital stock is being replaced by energy-saving
equipment and buildings, rather than permanently. (Long-term economic growth
rates are quite likely to be slowed down for other reasons, but they are
irrelevant to the present discussion.) Seen in that way, conservation helps
to buy time for discovering and developing alternative energy supplies. If
that time is not well used, however, an energy policy focused exclusively
on conservation might prove worse than useless, since it fosters the illusion
that action on the supply side is unnecessary, and in the short run may reduce
safety margins and weaken the capacity of the society to absorb emergency
shortages.

INTERNATIONAL ENERGY CONSUMPTION
COMPARISON--DISCUSSION

David O. Wood
Sloan School of Management
Massachusetts Institute of Technology

I am in agreement with the major points in Lincoln Gordon's analysis
and evaluation of the research results presented at this workshop. I also
agree with him that these results are suggestive concerning the causes of
intercountry energy consumption differences, and of the effects of differing
national policies affecting energy use. However, I am more pessimistic than
he as to their usefulness for policy formulation and analysis. For such uses
we require a complete decomposition of differences in terms of factors
affecting the structure of production and final use versus those affecting
intensity of use. Only then can we determine what policy instruments may be
appropriate and what their likely quantitative effects might be. The results
presented at this workshop do not, I believe, provide such a decomposition
of differences between the United States and any other country for any common use of energy.

The basic difficulty, it seems to me, is not sterility of analytical
technique, but rather serious limitations in comparable international source
data available for intercountry analysis and comparison. During our discussion we have identified the following factors which might account for
intercountry differences in energy use, including differences in:

- the prices of capital, energy, labor, and materials used to produce
  a specific homogeneous output,

- the vintages of the capital goods which are combined with energy to
  produce other goods and services,

- the quality of energy, labor, and other material inputs,

- the mix of products being produced and consumed,

- technologies being used in production,

- income levels,

- public policies which influence or regulate energy use,

- locational distribution of industry and population,

- climate and geography,

- culture and life-style.

To decompose intercountry differences requires us to measure and analyze data relating to each of these categories. The results we have been discussing are at best only partially successful in accomplishing this decomposition.

The three analytical approaches represented by the studies presented at the workshop including sectoral, input/output, and econometric analysis, tend to focus upon different categories. The sectoral studies tend to concentrate upon the differences in the energy efficiency of the capital stock required to produce a given level of output. Input/output studies concentrate upon the complete accounting for the sources and uses of energy, and on the direct and indirect energy content of a specific final good or service. Econometric analyses focus upon the role of relative prices in explaining intensity of factor use to produce a specified level of homogeneous output. In each instance assumptions are made concerning the influence of the other factors accounting for aggregate intercountry differences. Even the most successful analyses lump together in an "unexplained" residual many of the categories thought to be important.

Assuming that it is thought worthwhile to further refine analysis of intercountry differences in energy consumption patterns, what are the prospects for significant improvements in source data sufficiently detailed to distinguish the categories mentioned above? The prospects do not seem reassuring. I note that no participant from the statistical establishment has presented

information on plans and status of developing the kinds of international
accounts required. Even in the United States the development of regional
accounts sufficient for interregional analysis is not taking place. Thus
the prospects seem dim for extending the results presented in this workshop
to provide the more detailed analysis necessary for such comparisons to play
a significant role in United States policy formulation and analysis.

This suggests that an important recommendation for the workshop to make
is that additional resources be devoted to improving international accounts
for comparison of energy consumption patterns. The extent of such new data
development is open to discussion, but certainly for major energy using
technologies and products it would be appropriate to obtain more detailed
information on input factor prices, capital stock vintage, conditions of
deployment, and so on, in order to refine our understanding of the causes
of different energy use patterns.

In addition the extension of analytical methods of intercountry comparison of factor utilization patterns seems an important research objective.
As we use up the higher grade, cheaper resources, and as resource demand
increases in response to pressures for economic growth, the higher costs of
these resources will make their efficient use an increasingly important
national and international policy issue. Analysis and comparisons of intercountry experiences, especially comparisons with those countries whose particular circumstances place them in the forefront in developing technologies
and public policy for dealing with these issues, is most useful, and should
be an important objective of the research community represented by those
attending this workshop.

LIST OF PARTICIPANTS

Jack Alterman
Resources for the Future

Claude Anderson
Electric Power Research Institute

Michael Boretsky
U.S. Department of Commerce

Colin Brant
British Embassy

Steve Carhart
Brookhaven National Laboratory

Robert Crow
Electric Power Research Institute

Joel Darmstadter
Resources for the Future

Andres Doernberg
Brookhaven National Laboratory

Joy Dunkerley
Resources for the Future

Gideon Fishelson
University of Chicago

R. Eugene Goodson
Purdue University

Lincoln Gordon
Resources for the Future

James Griffin
University of Houston

William D. Hermann
Standard Oil of California

Eric Hirst
Oak Ridge National Laboratory

Charles Hitch
Resources for the Future

Scott Johnson
The Open University

Robert Loftness
Electric Power Research Institute

William B. Milam
Department of State

Joseph Parent
Institute of Gas Technology

Rex Riley
Electric Power Research Institute

Elinor Sachse
International Bank for Reconstruction
and Development (World Bank)

John J. Schanz, Jr.
Resources for the Future

Lee Schipper
University of California

Anne Schneider
European Communities Delegation

Sam H. Schurr
Resources for the Future

Joseph E. Smolik
Economic Commission for Europe

Robert Spencer
Industrial Consultant

Chauncey Starr
Electric Power Research Institute

Samuel Van Vactor
International Energy Agency

Ronald K. White
Stanford Research Institute

David Wood
Massachusetts Institute of Technology